DREAMING OF
Nirvana
OR THE NEXT
PEACEFUL
REVOLUTION

WILHELM HABERKORN

PAGE PUBLISHING, INC.
Conneaut Lake, PA

First originally published by Page Publishing 2021

ISBN 978-1-6624-7466-8 (pbk)
ISBN 978-1-6624-6113-2 (hc)
ISBN 978-1-6624-6114-9 (digital)

Printed in the United States of America

CONTENTS

ACKNOWLEDGMENTS

The author recognizes that a broad-ranging project requires lots of help from lots of people. Here are some who helped to create a much-improved product.

Thanks to all of them.

Michael Walters *was the one who performed the first complete edit and contributed many new perspectives to the book.*

Chuck Smith *accomplished the first complete reading of the book. His feedback helped a lot.*

James Kimball *contributed his thoughts on political correctness.*

Whitey Carpenter *helped in restructuring the table of contents.*

Walter Cox added his perspective on race issues.

Dr. Hermann Buchert *added a helpful general European and specific German perspective.*

Dr. Karsten Neinhaus *not only provided his German point of view but supported that with beneficial details.*

Grant Andreas Harrison Kumar, *my eleven-year-old grandson, expressing a progressive perspective on various political issues helped solidify my resolve to publish the book.*

ABSTRACT

The book tries to accommodate the fast reader with little time to spare by **highlighting keywords and critical sentences** and providing room for notes.

Dreaming of Nirvana or the Next Peaceful Revolution is a book about harnessing the private sector's full power. It is about transformative **solutions.** Solutions capable of addressing the United States' most significant **fiscal** and **social problems**.

> *The book attempts to map out a pathway toward fiscal and social sanity.*
>
> *Alternatively, our generation can continue to embrace fiscal and social insanity and burden future generations with our irresponsible legacy gifts.*

It does so by establishing **control over all aspects** of the **private sector,** and in doing so, it will elevate the private sector to be on par with the public sector.

The book sets the stage with a review of the current political and social environment—in particular, the Trump presidency, COVID-19, and the variety of responses to both events.

The book recognizes that both the public and private sectors are intertwined, complex, and interdependent in a **one-way** sort of way. Unfortunately, the public sector controls and manipulates the private sector to no small degree, primarily as a function of what party is in charge. Principally, there is no recourse for the private sector.

Being agile and flexible, the private sector optimizes under suboptimal, external conditions. What happens if we run out of agility and flexibility?

Given this dismal background, the book contends that the proposed solution, forming **an umbrella organization** for the **private sector**, will establish **parity** between both sectors and act as a **catalyst** for many needed **solutions**.

While the umbrella organization is the key, the book suggests **forming a viable third party**, the Independent Party, to answer many political problems.

This step would not be necessary under a cooperative political environment. Unfortunately, current Washington political behavior among Dems and Reps leave no other option to overcome the bickering, lying, blocking—in a word, "**politics**."

The book emphasizes the private sector primarily and addresses, secondarily, numerous pressing public sector problems. The book suggests specific solutions to the nation's most pressing issues, problems such as the following:

> *Federal budget deficits. The US operates under perpetual budget deficits while collecting consecutive record tax revenues.*
> *Trade deficits. The US accrues gigantic trade deficits regularly, both with friends or foes accompanied by critical supply chain dependencies.*
> *Racial tensions. The heated racial divide, as evidenced by periodic race riots, stems from dismal education and resulting economic inequality rather than systemic racism.*

Income inequality. The gap between high and low-wage earners keeps increasing.

Wealth gap. The gap between the rich and the poor keeps growing.

The book emphasizes the genesis for those thoughts as the Winston Churchill quote acted as a catalyst for the ideas presented in this book.

"The inherent vice of capitalism is the unequal sharing of blessings; the inherent virtue of socialism is the equal sharing of miseries."

One can infer that Churchill did not think capitalism had a problem. However, examining the "**unequal sharing of blessings**" part in 2020, the need for change is glaringly apparent—a change allowing capitalism to operate **more effectively** and contribute to a **more socially** just society.

The writing is on the wall; either capitalism is changing and becomes more compassionate, or the people will drift toward socialism, as exemplified in the 2020 elections.

The **simplicity** of the proposed solutions is in glaring contrast to the **complexity** of the problems addressed in this book. Astonishingly, forming two organizations is as **trivial** as it gets. There is no doubt that those two changes will put the country back on the right track and allow it to live within its means "again!"

The time of burdening future generations is finally over!
Now we need to comfort and embrace our failed surplus social engineers.

The book makes its case by highlighting significant **symptoms** and **paradoxes** that impact both the private sector and the public sector. Those chosen vehicles cover a broad range of currently essential topics ranging from national, global, social, political, educational, trade, immigration, security, and the like in an attempt to show the underlying complexity and interconnectedness.

Unfortunately, there are **no obvious** and readily **identifiable solutions** for any significant issues on the horizon going through all those problems and issues!

....

> *Neither public nor private sector has concrete*
> *and specific solutions to offer.*
> *What a surprise!*

....

And that is a very disappointing assessment.

On the bright side, the book offers some gems in the form of oxymorons.

The book dares to project the impact of all those proposed solutions, such as shifting several federal departments from the public sector to the private sector, in a Nostradamus-like fashion, for 2030 and 2050.

Finally, the book asks the **reader** to become **part** of the **solution** by adding or subtracting content and contributing to better solutions for subsequent republishing.

The intent is to collect all the feedback via a dedicated website and republish the revised book in periodic intervals.

Here is the collecting website: https://thenextpeacefulrevolution.com.

INVITATION TO PARTICIPATE

Let me express a sincere invitation to everyone who reads this book to also become part of it.

How might you ask?

You might want to contribute to the solutions and stop blaming everybody else!

Reading the body, you will find an ample number of empty spaces for notes, answers, added problems, and the like. There you can make your notations that can be complete deletions of some or all the ideas, followed by your improved set of solutions.

Let me make an essential point.

The book is an unequivocal success if a superior set of solutions replaces 100 percent of the offered content.

It is an oxymoron look-alike statement at first glance but turns out to be correct.

The underlying idea for the book is one of being a catalyst for vastly improved future content.

That thought follows the basic notion that many Independent brains' output is superior to a single one. Not based on science, but on belief!

Which brings me to the point of who should feel qualified to contribute.

Does it require a PhD?

Or can a high school dropout dare to offer his/her thoughts? The answer is quite simple; everyone is highly welcome to participate as my "King" Rudolf story will show!

Let me give you the basic, shortened version.

It is a true story that profoundly changed my perception of people.

> *In the early nineties, our family went on vacation in Barbados. We rented a Jeep and circumnavigated the island. On one of the many scenic stops, while gazing at the Atlantic, my wife and daughter caught a glimpse of "King" Rudolf for the first time. Two suspicious characters were climbing out of a hole across the street. Breathtaking scenery on one side, and not so pretty living quarters of two local bums, vagabonds on the other. What a contrast! And those two characters moved toward us as we were the only people in sight. The wife and daughter felt uneasy, and the son did not know what to do. Approaching us, "King" Rudolf started the conversation.*
>
> *"Can we assist you, and where are you coming from?"*
>
> *I responded, "We are visitors from the US and are trying to explore your beautiful island!"*
>
> *He responded with an unexpected phrase.*
>
> *"You must originally be from Germany, aren't you?"*
>
> *And then he showed his proper self.*
>
> *"My name is Rudolf King, and I'm a native of Barbados."*
>
> *He said that he visited Germany many times while he was in the merchant marines sailing the world. On layovers, waiting for his next ship to leave*

port, he did all those extensive excursions exploring Europe in general and Germany in particular.

He continued with a detailed thesis of European aristocracy and, in particular, the German version. And he knew his stuff! While he was pontificating, I was astonished about getting that much precise, correct information I knew or cared little about it. But he did! I was amazed, and he noticed that fact.

Then came the next bit of surprise.

"May I show you our Barbados hospitality and invite you to have a drink with me?" Seeing my reluctance, he continued, "Let me buy a new bottle of rum at the liquor store right there!" And he did!

So he surprised me again.

A Barbados bum, alcoholic, gives a thesis about European aristocracy and invites us all to have a drink of rum.

What a metamorphosis!

*He was transforming from the outward perception of a **bum** to **a self-educated European historian** to being a **philanthropist**!*

All of that in about forty-five minutes!

What a mind-opener and learning experience! And that is the moral of the story.

Valid and meaningful information can come from anybody or any level of society.

In the case of "King" Rudolf, it could not go any lower. Being a homeless bum is as low as it gets.

Kudos and a toast of rum to "King" Rudolf!

Here is the website that captures your input: https://thenextpeacefulrevolution.com.

Notes:

_____

_____

_____

_____

_____

PROLOGUE

Structurally, free economies consist of a public and a private sector.

One sector is structured, rigid, and not easy to change, while the other is innovative, flexible, and sometimes greedy, with severe unintended consequences.

Neither structure is perfect, far from it. There is another way to look at these structures in a much more exact way.

The public sector spends money, and the private sector generates wealth. What a system! We spend more money than we generate, and on top of it, our progressives want to spend even more!
All for the greater good of society!

Yet those structures produce the absolute best results known in human history over a broad laundry list of criteria in all their imperfections.

Optimum? No. But absolute best? So far, without any doubt.

We all know dividing the country into two structures is a gross simplification.
Why?

There is a gray zone, a zone where all the simplifications do not work. In some instances, the public sector typically makes money from selling its resources such as airwaves, gas, oil, fish, national parks, and the like.

So it does make some money!

In other cases, private contractors derive money from the public sector for their rendered goods and services. So it does create some revenues for the private sector.

That's why!

Centrally controlled, typically not free economies in socialist or communist countries have only a public sector as part of their economy.

Those economies typically focus on wealth distribution and fail miserably in the wealth creation part.

To no one's surprise, some of our progressive leaders hail them as role models!

Ergo, the observation of Sir Winston Churchill.

He best describes the contrast between both forms in his speech to the House of Commons in 1945.

"The inherent vice of capitalism is the unequal sharing of blessings; the inherent virtue of socialism is the equal sharing of miseries."

Churchill did not offer any solutions to the "*unequal sharing of blessing*" problem. He did not think it was a problem, yet in 2020, it needs some exploring.

Churchill was correct in general but incorrect in the specifics. The socialist Hugo Chavez of Venezuela managed to destroy a prosperous Venezuela with his socialist structure but made his daughter a billionaire.

Yes, corruption works exceptionally well in Venezuela and other socialist paradises.

But life is not simple, as China appeared with a mixed model for its economy. What they have is a centrally controlled dictatorship combined with the semiprivate sector for its thriving economy.

That model allows entrepreneurs to form new corporations with a soft touch of central communist party control.

Surprisingly, they seem to tolerate the existence of billionaires, unlike our Western progressives!

For starters, it brought three hundred million peasants out of poverty!

Yet for all its successes, capitalism is under attack from within. Not open but subtle, with high-minded motives aimed to seduce the naive and ignorant. No calls for revolution. No calls for uprising and violence—only an appeal to the kind nature in man. Only gentle requests for getting a VOTE in any kind of election. The new road to power seems to be slow and patient. The primary argument is for JUST income and wealth redistribution.

Seems fair!

— *Redistribute the wealth of millionaires and billionaires!*
— *Free college for everyone!*
— *Free health care for everyone!*
— *Tax the evil, large corporations!*
— *Close the wealth distribution gap! And while we're at it...*
— *Save the planet from overheating because of CO_2 emissions made by a mean-spirited, consumption-driven, capitalist society!*

Capitalism, by its very nature, is driven by individualism in the form of entrepreneurs and corporations.

And it relies on control provided by market forces. This "*non-system*" creates value, a high standard of living, and wealth for its participants like no other economic system, particularly exemplified in the United States.

With all its might and power capitalism creates, is there room for improvement? The socialists of the world would answer that question with a resounding YES. At the same time, the die-hard capitalists' answer is an equally emphatic NO!

Who is right, and who is wrong?

> **This book contends that capitalism is not running at an optimum and can be improved, not in the form envisioned by the socialist, equal distribution of all benefits, but by eliminating all or most of its inherent weaknesses.**

There is another not-so-original idea that has become relevant to capitalism or, in our case, the private sector.

Organize!

Typically, labor had to be organized in unions to get something done.

Now it is time for the private sector to get its ducks in a row.

Let us briefly dwell on historical references, starting with the good old days.

Notes:

_____

_____

_____

_____

_____

Good Old Days

The *"good old days"* provided specific adversaries for everyone to see and understand. It was simple then. Hitler, Mussolini, and the

Japanese Emperor tried to conquer the world, not because of matching ideologies but because it seemed an excellent idea to achieve a common end.

It is noteworthy that the Hitler party, NSDAP, had the label *social* embedded in its party name. We all know now that it was a different kind of social! Enough said. And it should be a warning for future generations to come. A label is just a label.

Social *does not imply the same for all lunatics in the world.*

In the end, all former attackers are now near the pinnacle of capitalism and trusted leaders in the free world—how time changes perspectives.
    So we find the biggest surprise of them all, the Germans.

While embracing their free economic structure, "Die Soziale Marktwirtschaft," the Germans have a balanced budget in the constitution and adopt the "Black Zero" as their annual federal budget target.

Could it be better?

Everyone expected that WWII was the last of the big wars. It was thus far, but the world's appetite for action did not stop there. Smaller scrimmages popped up here and there. And a new, more dangerous type of war appeared, the *Cold War*.

The world, while engaged in the *Cold War*, had clear delineations. East distrusted the West, and West distrusted the East.

The rift was ideology, socialism, and communism on one side versus capitalism or free enterprise or democracy on the other.
    The lunatics ran the insane asylum.

The distinction was oppressed societies versus free societies.

The choice seems obvious and straightforward, but it was not.

> *It was "nukes" by the thousands on either side that made that type of war dangerous.*

The end game was not "*win or lose*" but the destruction of the world!

> *What we had was insanity as ideology personified on either end.*

What was evident and clear to everyone then is not so obvious now. Nothing is cotton dry and clear-cut any longer. Ideologies also had physical borders—the Soviet Union and its allies had an "*Iron Curtain*" to prevent an influx of dissatisfied Westerners from entering their territory, or was it the other way around?

> *We know no one got shot going the Eastern route, but thousands died trying to go from East to West.*

The Cubans did likewise; all they got for their persistent adherence to their "*revolution*" was poverty on their end and a view of unlimited prosperity only hundred miles away. All their people could read and write, and they achieved the highest number of physicians per capita but, unfortunately, had no modern medical tools and drugs to help their people.

Another important lesson:

> *Education, by itself, does not produce anything. Having the freedom to apply the gained knowledge makes the difference.*

Two wars with no clear winner tested the resolve of the respective ideology in Korea and Vietnam.

President Reagan proved beyond any doubt that bankruptcy is a much more useful weapon than tanks, soldiers, and missiles.

No killing, but an obvious winner!

Giving three hundred million Eastern European people access to freedom seems a subtle side effect!

Okay, all of that was obvious.

Where to Go Next?

History is good, and it sometimes helps to avoid making the same mistakes over and over again.

But in our case, not so much!

So let's look at some of our dysfunctional system's more pronounced symptoms. And there are plenty of them to choose from; all we need do is open our eyes, look around, and take note of them.

It is that simple!

Notes:

_____

_____

_____

_____

_____

Symptoms

We all learned in school, quite early, that there are three branches of government. We elect the governing members of each part of the government, either directly or indirectly.

But do we?

Bureaucrats

Some of us even remember the function of each branch, but not all of us. It can be confusing if we look at the "*bureaucrats*," the ones who think they run the country. In their minds, they are the unelected fourth branch of government.

Bureaucrats are the steady hand that adds ability, loyalty, and zero political flavors.

While the fickle voters change the executives and legislators, the *bureaucrats* are the only constant. They work within the directive of any party, never mind what flavor.

Or do they?

Bureaucrats have never been confused with "*entrepreneurs*." Both happily reside on the opposite end of the "High Risk/Big Change versus No-Risk/No Change" continuum. We all know that we do not find too many *entrepreneurs* among the *bureaucrats*. There is virtually zero chance that any *bureaucrat* engages in entrepreneurial activities. They simply do not like change. To them, *entrepreneurs* are a pain in the rear end.

Now, in the most unlikely of unlikely events, an entrepreneur becomes the president, the chief executive.

The person who sets new and unusual policies, and on top of it, give a rat's ass about the ability and consistency of the vast imperium of *bureaucrats*.

How much love and acceptance would he get?

None, zero, zilch!

What tools do *bureaucrats* have at their disposal?

Many! They

- leak to the press and gather outside support or resistance,
- become a whistleblower to display their ethical ability,
- engage in slow resistance to prove to your coworkers and your newly elected bosses who are in charge, and
- guide with expertise and, better yet, with "scientific knowledge."

Bureaucrats don't mind changing from red to blue and vice versa, as long as there is a genuine and lifelong politician on the other end.

Politicians of either color are predictable and, as such, can be "*guided*" by experts, by the real power in government, *the bureaucrats.* Any color change requires a tiny pinch here and a slight twist there, and all is well as usual.

Nothing changes, but everybody is happy—most of all, the *bureaucrats.*

Voters, not so much, but who cares?

Notes:

_____

_____

_____

_____

_____

Enter the Election of Trump

A bold, *newly minted* politician dared to run for president of the United States of America! No regular training such as mayor, state rep, congressman, or US senator.

The swamp, i.e., *bureaucrats,* hated it and made him pay dearly. Anonymous leaks on any sensitive issue one can imagine.

The swamp formed alliances with the political establishment of the opposing party to remove him from office.

Spreading news of chaos and decent within the Executive branch. Anonymous, of course.

The swamp displayed their discontent openly in Congressional Inquiries.

Some swamp creatures fell into their sword for the greater good, trying to save the country.

The opposition—e.g., Democrats, resistors, leakers, and whistleblowers—acclaim them as *"patriots* and *national heroes."* They cleverly created the **Pelosi, Schumer, Schiff Theorem** to add legitimacy to their actions.

Unrelated facts or suspicions, combined into one or more sentences and uttered by either originator, will yield indisputable facts that nobody can question.

So much for political gamesmanship!

Unfortunately, the combination of *bureaucrats* and *politicians* can be a lethal one under the right circumstances.

Notes:

_____

_____

_____

_____

_____

Enter the COVID-19 Pandemic of 2020!

An invisible enemy, COVID-19, entered the field of battle in 2020.

The medical establishment had no vaccine, no proven treatment, and no recent experience with a global pandemic.

We can only manage the disease!

The only known remedies were behavioral, such as social spacing, wearing face masks, no face-touching, vigorous and frequent hand cleaning, and finally, extensive and constant media exposure.

The latter proves their scientific expertise to the county; the more you preach, the more compelling and believable your message!

The expected outcome was a "flattening of the curve."

Mind you, "flattening of the curve" does not reduce the area under the curve. It merely means stretching the area under the curve over a longer time horizon.

In plain English, the number of infections and casualties is stretched out but not reduced!

But none of the bureaucrats/scientists talks in those terms.

The principal goal: match patient rate with the medical system capacity

We all knew little about the behavior of COVID-19; it only potentially, fatally attacks more senior people, particularly those with a laundry list of comorbid conditions. It kills them at a significantly higher rate. The best news of it all: a high percentage of healthy and young people were asymptomatic.

So in all that mess, there was some good news.

Given those conditions, what were the chosen measures?

The *bureaucrats* or *scientists*, in this case, went to work with advising the *politicians*.

They went ahead and deployed the "scared shitless" strategy.

Scientists who knew extraordinarily little about COVID-19, but pretended to know a lot, came forth with *scientific models* that were supposed to project various possible outcomes of COVID-19. In ethical scientific fashion, they produced the *"worst-case scenario."* And for the worst case, it was, not surprising, casualty rates in the millions.

Prudently, you err on the side of caution while you support the perception of superior and not-to-be-questioned scientific knowledge.

Fatalities in the millions gets everyone's attention!

Now who wants to be responsible for killing Grandpa and Grandma?

Nobody!

And that number stuck in the minds of all politicians, left or right, with devastating outcomes.

It paralyzed them and took away any viable alternative. Any talk about alternative solutions was done and dusted.

Even though we know that all those numbers were scientific garbage, but garbage, nonetheless yet, who in his right mind wants to be a mass killer!

And most importantly, no other disease is a close match to any of those projected numbers!

Is it not ironic how a set of ivory-tower resident scientists specializing in a single scientific discipline can create so much damage?

There ought to be a reward for that.

"The Greatest Damage in History reward."

Some of the governors treated those projections like red meat.

"We will shut down our state until we have a vaccine!"

Good luck and good riddance as there is no state left to govern.

Let us look at some relevant casualty numbers for reference!

> *The COVID-19 death rate is about 160 per 100,000 US standard population.*
>
> *The suicide death rate is about 15 per 100,000 US standard population.*
>
> *The kidney disease death rate is about 15 per 100,000 US standard population.*
>
> *Influenza and pneumonia death rates are each about 15 per 100,000 US standard population.*
>
> *The diabetes death rate is about 25 per 100,000 US standard population.*
>
> *Alzheimer's death rate is about 30 per 100,000 US standard population.*
>
> *The cerebrovascular disease death rate is about 40 per 100,000 US standard population.*
>
> *The chronic lower respiratory disease death rate is about 40 per 100,000 US standard population.*
>
> *The accidents/unintentional injuries death rate is about 50 per 100,000 US standard population.*
>
> *The cancer death rate is about 150 per 100,000 US standard population.*
>
> *The heart disease death rate is about 160 per 100,000 US standard population.*

Adding all those non-COVID-19 causes together results in a vast number, while the COVID-19 rate stays at its original value. The bureaucrats/scientists opted to ignore all other causes of death to *focus on COVID-19!*

Unfortunately and ironically, ignoring those other threats does not make them disappear; far from it, it makes them even more extensive.

On the bright side, car accidents declined as travel was severely restricted.

Our *ivory-tower resident scientists/bureaucrats* should have recognized that the single-dimensional COVID-19 model is insufficient to address all the COVID-19-related issues. Even considering only medical problems, a multidimensional model is needed to come forth with a set of meaningful recommendations.

It is absurd to let a cancer patient die to save a COVID-19 patient.

So what were the proposed measures to stop COVID-19?
Shut down the entire country!
With that move, the problem took on an entirely new dimension.

A single-dimensional medical problem, COVID-19, exploded into a multidimensional medical and non-medical problem of previously unheard proportions. Monetarily, billions became trillions! Just like that!

The models created a five to ten trillion-dollar decision by shutting down the entire nation.
The magical shit hit the fan.
While the demise of COVID-19 patients was *mitigated*, PAUSING the life expectancy of all other medical issues seemed an innovative solution. Driving restrictions reduced traffic fatalities, but suicides, drug overdoses, all other medical causes received a significant boost.
How many? Who knows.

Governors selected economic winners and losers, typically large winners and small losers, with no supporting fact base.

Who can argue against protecting Grandpa and Grandma and, while we are at it, SAVING everyone from COVID-19?

No killing of COVID-19 patients here was the motto du jour! Would it not be more proper to minimize the overall death rate? COVID-19 happens to be only one part.

> *Other principal issues are to be resolved after settling who lives and who dies, like what businesses survive or fail!*

The Fed and Congress pumped money into the economy to soften the blow. And as usual, future generations are asked to foot the bill.

> *In the end, many primarily small companies will not survive, while many large companies receive a financial boost.*

In retrospect, under stressful conditions of a world pandemic, decision support and decision-making exposed our current power structure's apparent flaws.

> *Do not go to the ivory-tower residents for real-life solutions; you might experience some disappointment.*

There is ample room for improvement.

Notes:

_____

_____

_____

_____

_____

Enter the COVID-19 Pandemic of 2020 and Its Political Solutions

Throughout history, the US has stood up to challenging situations. Let us revisit the last one to understand better what the country did to cope with it. What was the last one?

9/11, of course. How can we forget?

On a bright, sunny day, a bunch of true believers killed themselves and thousands of others and woke up the entire nation.
Is that where the "woke" movement started?

A rude awakening it was!

President Bush was in office, and it did not matter that he was a Republican. The country responded as one, arm in arm: Republicans, Democrats, and Independents—a unification of politicians!
Can this be true? Yes, it was!
Race did not matter, religion did not matter, and country of origin did not matter.

All responded as Americans! One nation under God, indivisible…so it works!

With that response, all current adversaries knew a sudden change took place. Former squabbling individualists overnight appeared as a cohesive unit, backed by the most lethal military known to man.
Bin Laden must have moistened in his pants as he saw that sudden transformation!
And pay and still paying they did!
Now let us look at what the nation did in response to the COVID-19 pandemic.

By now, everyone knows that it is a real pandemic, and all our science, military, and eco-

nomic might, and unquestioned superiority in each one of them, are USELESS!

And that is a hard pill to swallow.

The country and the world had nothing to control the virus. Trump tried to be the cheerleader for the nation. He and some frontline physicians touted hydroxychloroquine but got some rude rejections from all sides, mainly the mainstream press and the ivory-tower scientific world.

So there was at least an effort to do something about it, but there was no love for it.

Even though the ever-present placebo effect could add a 20–70 percent cure rate, that's not true and acceptable science.

Is it?

What does a president do?

He listens to the scientist for advice and guidance. Here are the highlights.

There is an emergency need for bed capacity in NY and LA.

Supplied but never used!

We need ventilators by the truckload.

Supplied but found them to be particularly useful as killing machines.

We need an effective vaccine, which typically takes five years to develop.

Operation Warp Speed cut the projected time to about one year.

The skeptics say Trump cut corners.

Thus, the product is NOT acceptable.

Trump was lukewarm on masks; he treated it as a local responsibility and got hammered by the Dems and the "mainstream press."

Even though a CDC study of infected patients showed that70 percent wore masks.
Go figure!
Let us express it in engineering terms; the failure rate of 70 percent is UNACCEPTABLE *by any engineering standard.*
The gradual, surreptitious expansion of the virus prevented people from getting together and acting as a unit.

Whatever it was, there was no big bang like 9/11 that served as a unifier.

With time, the country polarized increasingly along with political persuasions.
And that is not reassuring!
We have a virus that does not discriminate along those lines, Dems or Reps; it has its own preferences: Grandpa, Grandma, and sick Aunt Sally! We have over 500,000 casualties racing to 600,000, and there is no 9/11 response on the horizon!
And politicking about this is a blood sport.

Thus, rather than helping each other to solve the problem, we want to score political points!

How sick is that?
Nancy, Chuck, what is your contribution to the virus solution?
The mainstream press has checked up on Trump's every move and diligently pointed out all his "errors," item by item.
Now how does that help to curb the pandemic?
The Dem's chief cheerleader Biden proudly orates, with great conviction, if chosen,

"I will have no blue states, no red states, only the United States."

Without any specifics, he continued that he could have saved 100,000 casualties (about the seating capacity of the Los Angeles Memorial Coliseum)!

He claimed to be the unifier but was unwilling to share his brilliant ideas with the Trump administration in a worldwide crisis.

All of Trump's opposition (mainstream press and the Dems) were unwilling to share their expertise with the president to become part of the solution.

In a pandemic, they wanted to be the critics!

Okay, we get that!
Just answer one question.
How many lives did you save being the vocal critic?
Answer: ZERO, ZILCH, NADA!
All we can say is, the COVID-19 response left a lot of room for improvement.

9/11 brought about the best in our nation.
COVID-19 revealed the worst in our nation.

Notes:

_____

_____

_____

_____

_____

Presidential Election 2020

We can't make up how that story ends.

Trump lost, and Biden won!

Trump lost on three accounts: first COVID-19; and second, the unified opposition of the mainstream press and the "Dems." That opposition was right in the open, and no big surprise.

What is the third reason?

Let's just say it. Silicon Valley and its generally liberally oriented corporations did their level best to defeat Trump. In particular, Google!

The big trillion-dollar digital giant Google, with its powerful search engine, influenced the election!

How, you might ask?

Cleverly, with manipulation of the search-result representation. Psychologist Robert Epstein says he can measure the impact of biased search results on an election outcome!

That's how!

He claims, for the country, an impact in the millions! Millions of votes, that is!

Is it far-fetched?

Not really!

Can it happen? Obama held the previous record of popular votes with 69 million.

The inspiring, dynamic, charismatic, energetic President-elect Biden, campaigning from his basement, set a record with 81 million, thereby trouncing Obama's record to smithereens!

It should be no surprise as a grandfather's image complimented all those attributes with a little touch of forgetfulness displayed in some of his sentences.

Smooth as silk!

That's the new way of capturing the attention of the nation!

Maybe, just maybe, somebody just overdid it a touch?

The ancient Greeks went to the Oracle of Delphi for answers, and modern Westerners consulted the Encyclopedia Britannia to do likewise.

All that has changed radically in the digital age, no more Oracle or Encyclopedia, both replaced by an instant source, a pearl of infinite-wisdom-possessing powerhouse, Google.
The nerds can finally tell everybody what to do!

We have questions; they got the answers.

Remember, we used to "xerox" to get a copy of a piece of paper. And now we "google" to get an answer to a specific question. We don't "xerox" any longer; we copy again, but we still "google!" So things change eventually.

We don't "Bing" or "Yahoo"; we "Google!"

Meaning Google can control the bias in any answer they care to give, and all of this to millions of users in more than 90 percent of all web searches!

Google responds now with specific phrases to any question, and that is where the rubber meets the road.

Google knows your IP address, zip code, and GPS coordinates—thus knowing your location and a whole lot more, whether you are in a swing state or not—and, with all that, can customize their answers in any shade they choose, blue or red.

So in the end, we have customized responses to millions of users—mind-boggling implications.

Given that Professor Epstein is correct and all conditions are plausible, elections and their influencing factors need a rethinking in the digital age.

It is not big money any longer but detail digital information that determines the outcome.

The voter is just a pawn in that game!

Now we must ask ourselves.

Is it wise to let a media giant determine the outcome without a declaration of intent in any of the responses given to voters, one voter at a time?

Or better yet, let the nerds tell you what to do!

And even more disturbing, all this free of charge for any political candidate **they** favor.

What are the implications?

Media corporations determine the winner de facto without casting a single vote.

We just had a remarkably close election in the swing states. Neither candidate won in those states by millions of votes.

Does this mean we, the nation, "googled" our presidential election away?

Somebody tells us how to vote, and we don't even know they did it!
It ought to scare the living daylight out of us!
Are we, collectively, lemmings?
More about Google in the chapter "What is the Solution?" under the subheading "National Security Issues."
Yet this is not the story. The story is

"Never Let a Good Crisis Go to Waste," a phrase popularized by Rahm Emanuel.

Well, we have a terrific crisis; it can't get much better than COVID-19.

Can it?

Here we are, the nation, and the world is under siege of a century pandemic, COVID-19. People are dying by the thousands, and our only defense is social.

The medical profession is under stress; we have no treatment nor vaccine.

Most of the nation is **frightened**, intentionally or unintentionally fanned by political speech and, in principle, confronted by two opposing philosophical solutions.

- *Our only social defense is individual responsibility!*
- *Our only social defense is a government mandate!*

And what is the biggest surprise of them all? In the most accessible country of the world, supposedly driven by individualism, the call for a ***government mandate*** carried the election!

By a small margin! Yet it had the day.

Surprise, surprise, more than one-half of the population yearns for central control in an emergency!

That observation should be a wake-up call!

Central control and a mandate for socialism are right around the corner.

Ironically, another set of factors turned out to be crucial—the concepts of **managing** or **solving** a problem. All the recommended social measures, such as masks, cleaning, and social distancing, are simply intended to **manage** the virus distribution.

Unfortunately, managing does not imply solving, eradicating, or making progress toward defeating the virus.

As for all the political implications, there again are two opposite points of view.

Biden proclaimed to be a much better **manager** of COVID-19.

He accused Trump of being inept in managing the virus.

While Trump continuously talked about having a vaccine in December to **solve** the problem,

> *the mainstream press and the Dems ridiculed Trump for his lack of realism.*

Now we know what convinced the voters, and it was not the person who proclaimed to solve the COVID-19 problem.

The message here is, don't bother solving a problem; managing is sufficient to win an election.

Come to think of it, that's what politicians do with all their other problems!

No solutions in sight, anywhere!

Back to Our Election!

Shamelessly, Rahm Emanuel's phrase guides our politicians.

> *While being politically very astute, they fail the test of unity and compassion for the fellow man during a pandemic!*

What is in store for us next?

We have a worldwide emergency, and the winning side, while calling for unity, acts divisive and uses Rahm's phrase as the winning platform.

> *While on the other end, in the president's office, decisive decisions occur to combat the virus and shift the balance of power away from the virus toward human victory.*

Ventilators—our shortage is converted to a surplus!

Thousands of beds added to increase hospital bed capacity!

Deploy an effective vaccine within less than one year through Operation Warp Speed!

The mainstream press and the opposing Dems ignore all those factors. None of both opposing forces offers any other viable solutions.

Only "valid and necessary" criticism!

Then the most unlikely news hits the nation! News flash!

The pharma giant Pfizer announces **one week after** the election the startling news.

*We have a 90 percent effective vaccine deploy-
able starting December 2020!*
*Fourteen days after the election, "Moderna"
announced a 94 percent effective vaccine!*

The stock market reached new highs.

Did this news vindicate Trump?

Hell, no, he was just predicting it!

Thus, the conclusions.

Even if you do all the right things to combat the virus, you get no credit!

Let's make an educated guess. The Pfizer CEO is not a friend of Trump's!

His Operation Warp Speed did produce results of a mind-boggling level. Unfortunately, he not only lost the election but does not get the credit!

*Nobody likes a wise guy and bully who claims
to be right all the time!*

The irony, he would have won, hands down, with Pfizer reporting the results one week earlier.

But they did not, so he lost!

There is another observation worth making. After Pfizer announced its COVID-19 vaccine success, it applied for emergency approval to the FDA. That FDA approval process took another 3–4 weeks, while COVID-19 set new records reaching about 3,000 casualties daily.

Operation "Warp Speed" hit a brick wall head-on and came to a screeching halt.

A bunch of bureaucrats and scientists had to give its stamp of approval. They took over the process of going through the data.
Mind you, not adding any value; just verifying, to be sure.
Indeed, we, the Advisory Committee on Immunization Practices (ACIP), got to cross every T and dot every I to be perfect under wartime conditions!

While COVID-19 did its thing, killing people indiscriminately at an accelerating rate, the bureaucrats and scientists did their thing: waste precious time!

Then the ACIP took a vote on the recommendation to deploy the COVID-19 vaccine: Seventeen in favor, four against, and one abstention.
One spineless expert could not even make up his mind?
Four of those brave experts are against deploying a vaccine with 95 percent efficacy!

What do they want?
Walk on water?

Let's summarize the facts to get a better picture. COVID-19 kills between 1,000 and 3,000 per day, and the vaccine killed none during the trials; and we, the experts, need three to four weeks to review the data to make up our minds!

What is the cost of perfection in terms of unfortunate souls?
It is at a minimum of about 20,000 and a maximum of about 80,000!

So much for bureaucrats being in charge!

Let's Go Back to the Presidential Election Aftermath

The apparent winner and new president Biden right away announced a new COVID-19 board that will scientifically solve all the COVID-19 problems.

What will that be? We must wonder—the obvious answer.

Mandate masks until we have a vaccine.

Or better yet!

Claim all credit as the full-scale deployment of vaccines will be during his administration!

Problem solved.

Notes:

_____

_____

_____

_____

_____

The Trump Presidency

Now we know Trump is a one-term president.

Did Trump accomplish anything?

The Dems and the mainstream press say no, not only no but absolutely no! And the rest of the world echoes that sentiment.

Why?

> **He damaged the nation's image and standing in the world in general.**
> **He bullied and intimidated our long-term allies, be it Europe, Japan, or Korea, and those relations are at an all-time low!**

The proof: All our partners did not mind seeing him go.

Most importantly and surprisingly, Trump was inept in dealing with COVID-19!

It seems all of Trump's opposition cannot separate the person and his diverse, sometimes rather crude and obnoxious behavior from his actual implemented policies. Trump, in that regard, is as predictable as it gets. He seems to like and enjoy the street fight, not physically but verbally and behaviorally. And the opposition and the rest of the world are unified in hating it—genuinely hating it! He says what he thinks! No polling of any nuance of his speech.

No, Trump speaks his mind, of the cuff, just like any Bubba having a brew or two.

No politician at that level ever dared to do that.

And to top it off, he can't even use that excuse; supposedly, he never had a drop of alcohol in any form!

Good or bad, that makes Trump be Trump!

We, as people, seem to expect the expected from our politicians. What are the specifics that Trump does not deliver:

- *the slick behavior*
- *the creative excuses*
- *the elegant bulletproof speeches*
- *the baby-kissing, and last but not the least*
- *the always-forgotten election promises*

The opposition and the world look for and expect a well-groomed politician in US president's role. Trump is none of it. He is a novice in the political arena, and it shows. Trump is crude, sometimes even juvenile in his treatment of his opponents, and has a knack for getting under the skin of everybody, friend or foe. The high turnover during his administration indicates only one thing; he wants to succeed at all costs. Never mind the cost of human connections he seems to sever at a previously unknown rate.

Destruction of all foes, and sometimes friends, appears to be a personal hobby of his.

And yet, with all that headwind, he does what is necessary to succeed. His policies create results for the good of the nation.

A German analyst calls all the broken pieces a "Scherbenhaufen," a pile of broken glass.

Let's try to understand the riddle called Trump. Why is it that 50 percent of the US electorate and 100 percent of the rest of the world hate Trump?

That's a lot of hate!

One of my reviewers simply said he lacks character! And even as a lifelong Rep, it caused him to vote for Biden. So having character was vital to him.

Maybe by way of example, we gain a better understanding. Let's look at the Pope, Pope Francis. He is beloved by virtually anyone, exudes kindness, caring, and leads by example.

The man is a saint, a saint who has plenty of character.

Yet in the church's most significant issue, the sexual abuse issue, he is either unwilling or unable to solve or even address the problem's policy side. He could, but he does not.

That said, having "character" does not solve problems.

Having no character but a desire to solve problems does.

The Trump Perception: Hero or Villain?

In the grand finale, Trump supporters from all around the nation, gathering at the nation's capital, Washington DC, aroused by Trump, storm the Capitol while shouting, "**Stop the steal**," and ransack the place. Five people died!

The political establishment is scared for their lives.

Security measures to protect them are inadequate as the capitol police prove to be grossly incompetent.

What is the answer?

Impeach Trump for a second time for inciting insurrection!

The second impeachment of Donald Trump revealed, not surprisingly, another dark side of party politics. Politicians, in this case, our elected lawmakers, seem to be willing and eager to create new laws but fail to adhere and abide by existing laws, and even more astonishing, the rights afforded to every citizen in our constitution.

Do they view themselves to be above the law?

The Senate trial revealed, quite astonishingly, that the Dems managers, led by a former law professor, Representative Raskin, wanted to convict the former President Trump by emotion only. At the same time, the defense stuck with precision to the fundamentals of existing law. All those officeholders swore to uphold the constitution, which they did not do.

They failed on two accounts.

First, not granting a sitting president his rights to free political speech, and second, voting guilty in a case that merely involved protected free political expression.

A guilty vote violated the constitutional rights of a sitting president.
This allows us to conclude that those senators violated their oath of office.

Thus, one can conclude that they are willing to create law but fail to adhere to existing law when it does not suit them or their purpose.

Law in impeachment trials becomes a pick-and-choose proposition!
And "First Amendment rights" are not afforded to former political opponents.

There is another apparent, uncomfortable question that begs for an answer.

What kind of law did former law professor Raskin teach his students? The style he tried to sell the country during the impeachment trial?

Ignore all case law and go by emotion only to convict a former president if it suits your purpose?
Thank god he quit teaching and advanced to become a lawmaker.

What the country and the world saw during the impeachment trial was partisan politics at its worst. Dems stayed united, while the Reps, the individualists' party, not surprisingly, did not.

We can suspect that all guilty votes hinged on the critical phrase uttered by Trump.

Go and "fight like hell!"

Even though all those hypocritical "guilty voters" extensively used that phrase in their political speeches.

All protected by the First Amendment!

Let's go back to our riots.

Contrast the left-wing riots throughout 2020 and bleeding into 2021. Professional protestors or, better yet, professional rioters without a cause were doing their thing day in and day out. Exercising their right to protest, and directly or indirectly supported by the local political establishment. Never mind the destruction of local businesses and the livelihood of law-abiding citizens.

What is the answer?

The right to protest seems to outweigh the rights of law-abiding citizens!

Let's get that straight.

Protesting, rioting, and looting inside the Capitol is an insurrection, while doing the same to average citizens is just protesting, rioting, and looting!

There seem to be two standards, one for the powerful and one for the ordinary people.

Let's go back to the Washington incident and try to understand why they shouted, "**Stop the steal!**"

For one, Trump in the post-election period claimed a stolen election but could not support his claims through the court system. He looked for the hidden devious action but failed to see the apparent difference, **mail-in voting**.

The 2020 election, surprisingly in a pandemic, mustered 26 million more voters than in 2016, thereby setting new voter turnout records.

We know from the initial vote tallies that Trump won the traditional in-person vote and Biden surpassed Trump in the mail-in votes.

What is the problem?

Where is the "steal?"

Steal *may be the wrong word. Maybe "lack of control" is a better description.*

Let's contrast in-person voting with mail-in voting to highlight the differences.

In the in-person process, we know for sure WHO *voted and the voter cast a vote* SOLITARILY.

We don't know for sure WHO *voted in the mail-in process, and we don't know if the voter or* SOMEONE ELSE *cast a vote.*

So we are not sure or confident in one of the most critical actions a democracy has to offer. We ask the electorate to transfer the people's power to the elected, and we are not sure! To top it off, we are surprised that some people are not too confident about the process.

Did anybody "harvest votes"?

We have to ask ourselves, do we want such a "lack of control" in close elections or any election? Are our elections governed only by an "*everybody can vote*" election process?

> *Do we prefer to collect votes, any vote, in buckets? The one with the fuller bucket wins.*

The Washington riots and the insurrection were preventable and would most likely not have happened in a strict in-person voting process.

Trump, the villain/hero, struck again!

The preceding created another previously unheard action among our mighty social-media companies.

Twitter is the leader of the social-media insurrection.

Besides Dems, Twitter cast Trump as a villain. For the Dems, the previously used but unsuccessful playbook of impeachment seemed like an excellent repeat idea, and Twitter chimed in with their punishment method.

> *A sitting president of the United States gets a "life sentence."*

The most powerful man in the world gets the boot by Jack Dorsey.

Who is next, Vladimir Putin? "Jacky Baby," that would be a daring move!

The man who used Twitter for most of his communication to his base for the last four years and the free world leader is banished. Other social-media companies follow in lockstep. The reason? Twitter wants to prevent any future incitement of conservative riots, insurrections.

They want to be the guardians and protectors of democracy itself—an admirable and challenging gesture from a private enterprise.

> *Anyone still doubting the power of social-media companies!*

Trump, the villain/hero, struck again!

One of Trump's primary campaign promises: build a wall on the Mexican border and let Mexico pay for it!

He built 450 miles of wall, slowed down the caravans of illegal entry to a crawl, and paid for it through budget gymnastics.

On top of it, he converted NAFTA to the USMCA, which indirectly covers the wall's expenses.

The resulting lack of cheap labor caused labor shortages in the US and increased labor costs in the US during the booming Trump economy.

There is a cause-and-effect relationship between illegal immigration and labor costs on the macroscale.
Surprise, surprise!

Trump, the villain/hero, struck again!

On the foreign policy front, Trump tried to resolve the North Korean nuclear problem via personal diplomacy. He met the dictator twice, tried to sell prosperity for the North Korean people in exchange for nukes, but got a rude rejection from the dictator. The dictator did not see any benefit for himself as he already enjoys all the creature comforts Trump tried to sell. As for the North Korean people,

---

dictators do not care how their people live.

Trump, the villain/hero, struck again!

And there was the trifecta of NATO, US Troops, and the US-EU trade, done Trump's way! Not too surprising, all handled in a one-way sort of process.

"My way or the highway," as the saying goes.

Did Trump gain new friends among his European allies?

No, and an emphatic NO is the answer.

Did Trump have any valid reasons to behave that way?

Yes, and emphatic YES is the answer.

Let's review the specifics to see if Trump was right, not with his behavior but with the specific issues.

Let's review the NATO issue.

The US share of NATO defense expenditures is about 2/3 of the total while spending about 3.42 percent of GDP.

The majority of NATO members do not reach the agreed 2.0 percent of GDP target.

Thus, asking each member to carry their respective agreed load was appropriate!

The US troop deployment issue.

Trump used the US troop deployment to places like Germany as his "Trump Card." He wanted to get paid for his troop deployment, which did not endear him with most Europeans.

Historically, the national security of European nations was the US free-of-charge service since WWII.

Why change now?

The perpetual US budget deficit may quality for an answer.

And last but not least, the US-EU trading arrangement.

Trump did not like the status quo of financially getting hosed by friends and allies.

The US provided free national security and financed European prosperity with a perpetual trade deficit. Trump questioned that historical arrangement in his crude and endearing way.

Rather than entering protracted negotiations, he opted to threaten trade tariffs on essential products to get everyone's attention.

He got their attention!

Did he make friends? The resulting disapproval of nearly 100 percent speaks for itself.

Trump, the villain/hero, struck again!

In summation, he failed everywhere and accomplished nothing!

That is one perspective, but not an objective one.

While it is true that Trump was a disrupter, troublemaker, and all the other attributes brought to bear by the mainstream press, yet despite all that headwind, he can claim astonishing accomplishments.

And to no one's big surprise, he does not even get any credit for those.

What Are Trump's Most Significant Achievements?

Operation Warp Speed is his single most significant accomplishment, bar none.

Trump recognized that COVID-19 put the world on a warlike footing quite early and proactive measures are required to defeat the virus.

*It was clear that all the **social remedies**, in particular masks, would not solve the problem; it would only **manage** it.*

Trump's solution was being a **businessman** and **entrepreneur** at its **best**. As commander and chief, he used the military for logistics aspects, as chief executive, the private sector for developing a viable vaccine in the form of six private enterprise channels, and most importantly, funded pre-production of vaccines during the preapproval phase. All done to shrink the time horizon to a bare minimum for several viable vaccine options. He was harnessing all possible resources to achieve an end.

It made the "development horizon of less than one year" a reality.

How can we best express the magnitude of this accomplishment? Assuming a typical five-year vaccine development horizon, then we have saved four years with a world casualty level of about 1,000,000 per year, give or take.

Mind-blowing numbers! World War II-type numbers! In the end, Trump's Operation Warp Speed will have saved multimillions of lives worldwide.

Yet, even after the successful launch of vaccines, some unteachable morons in the mainstream press and the Dems still accuse him of COVID-19 mismanagement!

Go figure!

Does he get credit? No!

Trump ought to get a Nobel prize for that accomplishment!

No single individual in humanity's history has saved that many lives in such a short time frame!

Let's get that straight: Trump beat the virus and saved millions of lives, and he lost the election being lukewarm on masks, i.e., unable to manage COVID-19!

What does that say about the electorate?

A close second to Operation Warp Speed is the new approach to the Palestine problem.

Brokering Arab-Israel peace deals will, in the long run, bring Palestine to the negotiation table and undoubtedly solve the problem.

Who would have thought that the phrase **"the enemy of my enemy is my friend"** would be the solution!

Genius!

The mainstream press duly ignores this game-changing accomplishment.

Does he get credit? No!

The third most significant accomplishment is the dismantling of a vast number of meaningless regulations.

The bureaucrats did not like that; it reduced their power bases but cranked up the Obama economy.

"Don't take my work; just ask Obama!"

Unfortunately, COVID-19 came and brought the booming economy to a screeching halt.

Does he get credit?

*No, as he hands over a country in a **"Trump recession"** to Biden.*

What Are Trump's Most Significant Disappointments?

Let's rummage through the "Scherbenhaufen" and analyze what people prefer in a politician, any politician. Listening to many sources both here and abroad, "character" and "predictability" are two terms people seem to yearn for in a US president.

What is character? Some definitions contain a laundry list of trustworthiness, respect, responsibility, fairness, caring, citizenship, and empathy.

Tough standards to meet, and Trump did not.

Trump prided himself as a dealmaker, and if there is one thing a dealmaker cannot be, it is to be predictable, and Trump was not.

Now we established Trump is an unpredictable character!

Now that we know Trump did not, out of curiosity, who most probably meets those standards? Best guess...

Career politicians who do not take any risks and poll every word they ever utter in public.

That's who!

Back to Trump's Disappointments!

Does he have any?

It would be naive and somewhat closed-minded to see only the bright and vividly colored side. Like everybody else, the man has flaws, and we ought to recognize those and point them out.

Let's give it a try to single out his three most significant disappointments.

Interestingly, his single most significant accomplishment is also his single most considerable disappointment!

COVID-19, the killer pandemic!

Why, you might ask?

There are two reasons.

As previously mentioned, Trump was lukewarm on masks, and he did not issue firm national guidelines to wear them and do the social distancing.

He surrendered his responsibility to state and local officials.

The Dems and Biden ceased on that and won the vote.

Second, Operation Warp Speed produced the vaccine in record times but reduced itself to snail-mail speed by deferring the "**Shot in the Arm**" to the states.

Again, he made the same mistake counting on state and local officials.

Big mistake!

The magnitude of delivering about 200 million vaccines requires a new temporary infrastructure the states could not provide.

The Dems and Biden have already started to cease on that flaw and will claim to be "the vaccinators."

What was his second most significant disappointment?

The failure to make the transition from a party leader to an all-inclusive president!

The hostile environment on both sides of the aisles in congress is one reason. And the relationship with the mainstream press and Dems never softened to any degree. Nancy and Chuck did not accommodate him, ever! So there is blame for everybody to share. Yet he was the president, the man in charge. With that position comes the most significant share of responsibility.

Sorry, Mr. President!

Finally, what was his third most significant disappointment?

His dealing with foreign leaders.

Diplomacy was an inconvenience in his dealings with the various foreign leaders.

He openly preferred to be blunt, demanding, unyielding, and results-oriented.

Successful in some cases, as NATO bank accounts swelled immensely, and NAFTA morphed into USMCA.

Yet most, if not all, foreign leaders did not shed any tears after his defeat.

Biden ceased on that with his compassionate and accommodating approach in a 180-degree reversal.

In summation, Trump, the troublemaker and bully, changed the political landscape to a significant degree. History will provide the final judgment.

What Did All the Trump Stuff Prove?

Politics is a dirty game, and it gets more contaminated by the minute.

Let's look at the second impeachment and evaluate its validity with that thought in mind. What are the underlying requirements for any elected office?

First, uphold and defend the constitution, and second, judge everybody equally.

Interestingly, rules and laws are viewed as somewhat flexible tools of the trade by the career politicians on either side of the aisle.

At first glance, the phrase "fight like hell" can be viewed as the catalyst for all that followed on January 6 in Washington. However, and unfortunately, many politicians favor that particular phrase. It fires up any crowd, be it Reps or Dems. So we know it is part of everyday political speech! And there is another noteworthy and critical aspect.

The First Amendment protects such political speech for anybody, be it Dems or Reps, citizens or President!

And yet, despite all those crucial protections, the Dems found it necessary to impeach the president. In their eyes, the president did not make a political speech. Using the phrase "**fight like hell**," his speech was the prologue to the following insurrection, even though he closed with another phrase, "**Go and protest peacefully**."
Then came the trial in the Senate.

It is essential to recall that every one of those senators swore an oath to uphold and protect the constitution.

The accused, the sitting president, is charged with inciting insurrection during a rally of supporters doing what any politician does best: making an inspiring political speech under the protection of the First Amendment.

Yet he is charged!

Then the true crime takes place committed by all those senators voting "guilty." What's the crime? The "guilty" voters, in their callous political efforts, violated their oath of office to uphold and protect the constitution. Like it or not, even a president can make an uncomfortable political speech under the rights afforded to him by the First Amendment. All those "guilty-voting senators" should know as most of them carry the burden of knowledge signified by a law degree.

Those senators wanted to remove a sitting now-former president for activity protected under the First Amendment, all of that open to the public on national television.

What is the remedy?

Engage in a never-ending cycle of political retribution? Obviously not. There is only one conclusion:

The political establishment is highly dysfunctional and warrants a significant makeover.

Politicians of any stripe are not into solutions to our numerous problems; they only prefer to manage those problems.

The election of 2020 showed, without any doubt, that Reps who adhere to individualism show up and vote in person, while Dems, who believe in collectivism, prefer to vote amass by mail.

Guess which method canvasses more previously untapped voters?

Unfortunately, those Bible-thumbing and gun-toting individualists get angry if they collectively feel they got disenfranchised.

The January 6 incident at the Capitol might be the canary in the coal mine.

As for our friends and allies, there is a substantial financial and national security dependency among partners of Uncle Sam.

The US allies on either side of the pond strongly prefer an America that adheres to the historical status quo. All is perfect from their perspective—minimum contributions to national security for NATO payments and maximum perpetual trade surpluses.

Anyone who questions that comfortable status must be a populist, one who appeals to ordinary people and not to high-and-mighty intellectuals.

Never mind the perpetual US federal budget deficits and the associated deferment of payments to many future generations to come.

For instance, we, Germany, are fiscally responsible and adhere to our "Black Zero," no matter what.

Let the Yanks elect a better president to fix their problems.

Who needs enemies if you got allies and friends!

As for exiting WHO, Paris, and Iran deals, none is worth the ink. Why, one might ask out of curiosity?

WHO showed its uselessness in dealing with the most critical worldwide health challenge since its inception. First, it covered up for China, and second, it tries to uncover COVID-19 origin in China one year after the pandemic's start!

None of the COVID-19 solutions came from WHO!

Who needs those incompetent and useless bureaucrats!

The Paris Climate Accord gives India and China, the biggest polluting countries, a free pass until 2030. China, the second most powerful economy globally, is deemed to be a "developing country."

China, "the developing country," aims to surpass the US as the dominating military and economic superpower within the next ten years!

What we have as a consequence is an oxymoron.

A superpower "developing country!"

The Iran nuclear deal assures a slow pass for the Ayatollah to go nuclear.

Having a guaranteed nuclear Iran in thirty years does not solve anything!

Do We Have a Dysfunctional Government?

Like no other recent period, the Trump years magnified all the kinks in our government. Numerous indicators point to a widening of the chasm between both parties. All the problems of the nation remain in place, untouched by either party in power. There is no point in going through a detailed regurgitation of all those vast issues. The fact here is simple; no solutions are forthcoming any time soon under the current configuration. Why?

Let's begin with the underlying premise.

Washington these days is all about gaining, retaining, and defending power, and it is not about doing the nation's business for the good of the nation and its people.

Nobody even pretends to solve any of the nation's biggest problems.

All players, Dems or Reps, made their respective contributions. Let's look at some of these events to gain a better understanding of the underlying causes.

What were the worst offenders? Here we have a clear winner.

COVID-19 and all the political ramifications!

What did our politicians do? Rather than working together, they engage in political gamesmanship. Unlike 9/11, which united the nation, COVID-19 divided the country.

Sadly, a century world pandemic is a convenient tool to enhance political power.

One faction protests, riots, and loots to make themselves essential. Another faction storms the Capitol in support of their president, all during a pandemic, while people die daily of COVID-19 by the thousands.

For some reason or another, it had to be political because of the upcoming presidential election. There were clear delineations;

reaching the pinnacle of power is more important than helping and healing a desperate nation.

Sadly enough, it worked.

The Dems got the ultimate reward, the grand prize, the presidency of the United States. How did that happen? Let's look at the entire process from an electorate perspective.

Historically, the US electorate shifts its preference for a leader or party in an unpredictable fashion. The Trump election and the Biden election are a case in point. What did occur?

In the Trump case, a shift away from a novice politician who kept his promises with his policies but failed concerning his character and dealings with the press, opposition, and foreign leaders.

In the Biden case, the landslide election of a leader clearly past his prime, as evidenced by his difficulties finding the right words when he desperately needs them.

So the electorate is also desperate to find solutions to the problems of the nation. Did they? Early indications are, they did not.

Spending $1.9 trillion on a COVID-19 relief package where only about less than 10 percent is COVID-19-related does not qualify as a serious move toward solving the deficit-spending problem.

Again, pleasing its power base is more important than solving the nation's problems!

What are other examples of a dysfunctional government? You guessed it, the dual Trump impeachment.

In each case, a single sentence or phrase uttered by the president was a sufficient catalyst to put the nation through a wringer.

We have to ask ourselves, Are we better off as a nation having gone, not only once but twice, through the impeachment spectacle?

Probably not!

And to top it off, we as a nation do not know how to vote reliably and acceptably for all parties.

We, the Dems, claim to do all the shenanigans for the good of the disenfranchised voter, but in truth, we are willing to apply any means possible to shift the advantage in our favor.

It is not about winning fairly, but it is about winning at all costs and gaining power.

The most disturbing indication of a dysfunctional government presents, to no one's great surprise, the COVID-19 vaccination progression. What are those indicators?

With its Operation Warp Speed effort, the Trump administration made the early availability of various vaccines possible. While they made mistakes on the distribution end, there can be no doubt about the success on the development and acquisition end. Buying eight hundred million doses of yet-to-be-developed vaccines from various sources was historical and monumental by any measure.

That move saved millions of lives.

It made early mass vaccinations possible.

What did the Biden administration do to "carry the ball into the end zone"? They criticized the COVID-19 shortcomings of the Trump administration. Okay, we should get that. However, without Operation Warp Speed, the Biden administration would not be able to vaccinate the nation.

They have difficulties saying thank you to the Trump administration in the country's name.

The chasm between Dems and Reps widens during a pandemic, a time of dire need to unify for the nation's good and its people.

And it also vividly illustrates that—to steal a phrase—"power corrupts and absolute power corrupts absolutely."

What do all the preceding suggest?

Let me make a prediction, given zero change to the current political configuration,

> **"The US will have a man on Mars before the nation reaches a balanced federal budget again!"**

Sadly, we have only one viable option.

> **Revamp the political infrastructure to go back and do the people's business for the good of the nation and its people.**

Notes:

_____

_____

_____

_____

_____

THE VACCINATION DILEMMA

By now, nearly everyone around the globe knows, COVID-19 is in a war-like setting against humanity. The number of casualties thus far is ample proof; a different global war is taking place right now against a devious virus that continually changes, morphs, and adapts to changing conditions. Humanity has gained the upper hand despite all that cleverness by developing and deploying several COVID-19 vaccines of nearly miraculous efficacy and virtually non-existent side effects.

Yet, while having the unquestioned solution at its disposal, humanity shows an unwillingness or lack of leadership to defeat the virus. Why?

The best answer for the United States is the price of freedom. In a free society, free people can make individual decisions that are not necessarily in the best interest of the entire society, and they do. While most people make the correct decision, get vaccinated, and protect everyone else, a significant portion of the population is unwilling to do likewise. Why?

There is a laundry list of reasons cited by them in support of their decision. They range from religious, intellectual, pseudo-intellectual, distrust, conspiracy, and the like reasons to support their specific version of logic.

Numerous highly educated pseudo-intellectuals cite my favorite example.

Before we get vaccinated, we like more data and have a properly approved vaccine.

One can infer that those people have the ultimate trust in the scientific process and government agencies even though those tools are here to predict the actual outcome. Anecdotal information such as millions moving toward billions of vaccinations are not acceptable!

All we know, those reasons are multiple but have one common denominator:

They fail to see the individual's required contribution to the protection of the entire population.

We have a significant percentage of our population that is not interested in the common good. Protect everyone else! They are only interested in themselves.

That is one side of the story.
What about leadership?
There is none in this war!

We have no general who is willing to get the job done with the least number of casualties.

People are still dying day in and day out. At the same time, 99.999% of vaccinated people survive any COVID-19 infection.

What is the answer?

Maybe we should put the unrestrained ability to be a Moran in a free society on hold during a pandemic.

Notes:

_____

_____

_____

_____

_____

The Racist USA

Is the US racist?

Many groups, factions, political persuasions say yes. Yet cooler heads argue no.

What is it!
And what are some of the supporting facts?
On the macroscale, we know that there was a civil war that abolished slavery. However, all of that did nothing about discrimination. The civil rights movement ended that!
Or did it?
We know that progress is hard to come by, and it shows in period explosions of race riots of the sixties, Rodney King, and now, George Floyd.

We know inner-city kids get lousy or no education with no prospects of supporting themselves in the future!

Gangs offer the best available alternative for being part of something. The likelihood of ending up as a criminal doing jail time is enormous.

Growing up without a father as part of our government's progressive welfare system is not helpful.

On top of it, there are all the do-gooders, like Al Sharpton, who make an excellent living touting the race card. While Al promotes his own horn, every opportunity he gets, nothing changes for the poor inner-city kids. Al is not into solutions; he is uncovering problems, particularly White issues, to support his highly profitable race-inequality business model.

At least Al Sharpton is in the open, and his motives are easy to see.

> *More difficult to spot are the college-educated protestors, primarily White and naive, willing to riot, destroy, and loot as part of progressive post-graduate studies.*

Those kids will not have to go back to inner-city living in neglected neighborhoods after burning down mostly minority-owned businesses. No, plush areas are in their future. For all we know, they might end up in politics.

After proving their skills in physical destruction, they are now sufficiently qualified to do intellectual damage. And kick it up another notch.

Become a politician!

Even more tricky is the financial support for all those professional protestors. Who does it, and what are the underlying motives? Chaos and destruction are not beneficial for those living in those neighborhoods, but it can be to those who understand the broader ramifications.

May we dare to utter the dirty words "financial speculation"!

> *Here we have it; predictable chaos can be very profitable! Unfortunately, not for the "smut's" doing all the damage.*

Notes:

_____

_____

_____

_____

_____

Law and Order

We live in a country based on law and order and are also part of the world's most accessible country. We all have rights embedded in the US Constitution. Unfortunately, that freedom comes at a price.

People will do stupid things, not necessarily criminal, but foolish, nonetheless.

A small percentage will do unlawful things, while the majority tries to live within the boundaries set by our laws.

The mob destroys and mutilates statues and monuments at will. Some institutions proclaim not to intervene. Our civilization is destroying itself by yielding to the throng of anarchists.

Remember ISIS blowing up archeological treasures in Iraq and Syria.

Like them or not, ISIS had a clear goal: go back to Mohammed's time and live by the Quran's strict rules.

Ignorant young men fought for the honor of becoming martyrs with clearly defined rewards of the flesh.

Our newly minted anarchists have no such guidance. They simply want to destroy and loot and ruin without having a clear, achievable goal or mission.

What do we have in contrast?

> *We have a misguided bunch of professional protesters who do not know what to do with their lives.*

Thus, protesting has become their job!

What is different here?

No religious belief, for sure.

But more importantly, we simply have a bunch of crybabies who think they are changing the world without having any notion of how and to what.

They only live by one fundamental concept: hate everybody who created the world's greatest country while having no sharp vision of a better society.

Only destruction!

> *And sometimes a "free" TV gotten via looting as a souvenir for future remembrance.*

The behavior of neglecting laws or not adhering to rules is most diverse in free societies. Totalitarian societies do not have the same problem; they do act and sometimes without cause. And for that, it can be admired by socialists like Bernie Sanders.

He disliked millionaires and billionaires, but he changed his rhetoric to billionaires since he became a millionaire.

Has he undergone a capitalistic transformation?

Bernie admires the achievements of Castro's communist Cuba! Yes, there are positive things in those countries, but at what cost?

The trifecta Trump, COVID-19, and George Floyd protest brought to bear an unusual idea.

Defund the police!

> *For the first time, the political left is proposing a cost-cutting idea.*

Very surprising!

And socialists like Alexandria Ocasio Cortez, aka AOC, jump right on it to support it.

Not very surprising!

Typically, she is only for spending money!

Not very surprising!

Intellectual powerhouses, such as NY Mayor DeBlasio, implement such an idea.

Not very surprising!

None of the originators seems to have thought about the implementation and its consequences.

Not very surprising!

The idea at its face is an excellent idea if, and only if, all criminals become law-abiding citizens.

No efforts along these lines exist.

If we have a free society, all perps are presumed innocent until proven guilty, meaning someone must do the proving.

Or, without police, ask the criminals to turn themselves in!

It is more cost-effective that way.

Let us consider another angle. A group of people who engage in peaceful protests, and on the side does a little rioting and looting, propose to *"defund the police."* Looks pretty logical from their perspective—*a tiny minority*. Let the perps define the rules.

Rule #1: Defund the police, thus no cops and no jail.

Our law-abiding citizens, *the vast majority*, disagree! For them, no new rule necessary.

Rule #2: We got plenty of laws to protect our community.

Let us face it; all the current and earlier race protests and riots originated for good reasons. Some specific members of the police force did terrible things in the name of protecting our citizens. So there is a good reason for the change. However, the one called for by the "*Black Lives Matter*" group is not one of them.

What do we want?

Dead cops!

When do we want it? Now!

Under those conditions, it is hard to imagine that anyone wants to become a police officer.

Notes:

_____

_____

_____

_____

_____

Politicians

The US has structural problems neither party, Democrat or Republican, is willing or able to address. So they continue to ignore it and only mention it in "*small-talk, cocktail-party chitchat*" or on the perpetual campaign stump—issues like the astronomically growing "*national debt*" or the lack of a "*balanced budget*" or the persistent "*trade deficit.*"

Politicians like to spend. And there is no clear distinction between both parties.

Dems are more for quick social payments, while Reps are more for more national defense.

Neither side offers permanent structural solutions. And both have Washington speech in their vocabulary.

Savings, in amusing Washington speech, is a reduction in the growth rate of spending.

All proposed new expenditures are *"paid for."* How? Typically, a tax revenue projection over the next ten years.

Nostradamus could not do that, but Washington politicians can.

For an expert politician in Washington, fiction is a mandatory skill, specifically in fictional numbers. The only requirement: *Communicate your nonsense with a straight and trusting face.*

A new breed of politicians is coming to the forefront—young, brash, self-confident, inexperienced, and female. Their focus is primarily on creating an image in the digital world—million Twitter followers mandatory!

For the most part, it is good that one of the male bastions, politics, is balanced with an equal female presence. Yet new and different does not mean better in all instances. A group of four have named themselves "the Squad" and brought attention to themselves in various ways.

Let us look at some musings provided by the Squad, and you be the judge.

One of the members, AOC, ventured into the field of macroeconomics.

AOC quote: Capitalism assumes scarce resources, but now we approach infinite resources. Therefore, it is a matter of fair distribution.

Given she is correct, the Nobel Prize in economics is the next plausible step.

Unfortunately, an astronaut sitting in the space station orbiting earth sees only a finite sphere with a thin air layer.

To him/her, everything is finite!

Macroeconomics is not her only expertise; AOC shines as well in microeconomics!

Recall Amazon's efforts to set up another headquarters in New York. Trying to add 50,000 well-paying jobs to the NY tax base at Amazon calls for some concessions on NY's part. Reduced tax rates over a ten-year horizon were the answer. AOC had severe problems with the arrangement. She protested and voiced her opposition with compelling logic.

> *"NY should not give concessions to the rich and powerful Amazon Corporation. NY can spend those larger funds in more meaningful ways!"*

She was oblivious to what those funds were: reduced taxes, not actual money. Again, AOC's flawed insight is quite compelling, particularly to her one million Twitter followers.

We know how that sad story ended. Amazon bailed out of the arrangement, and NY can spend all the *"hot air"* in more meaningful ways.

Bless her heart; such insights sound so great while serving drinks. Why do they fail in real life?

AOC also has an opinion about defunding the police. What a surprise! The increase in crime, mostly shooting innocent people, prompted another excuse.

> *High unemployment causes poverty, which results in the shoplifting of food, a justified crime! Maybe the perp should not use a loaded gun!*

Let us go to the next member of the Squad, Ilhan Omar of Minnesota. Her new specialty also is economics. So she goes beyond her degrees in political sciences and international studies.

> *Rep. Ilhan Omar called for dismantling economic and political systems that serve as a "system of oppression."*

Those profound utterings used Apple phones and the Twitter platform to get the word out. I wonder how she plans to dismantle Apple and Twitter.

Be careful; do not shoot yourself into the foot: no Apple, no Twitter, no message to any comrade.

Worst of all, no political future!

It is astonishing that an immigrant from a failed country, Somalia, stays in a time warp, pretending to talk about America but seeming to think about Somalia.

Does she still suffer from her tragic experiences in Somalia?

Give her a break, and she has suffered enough! Just do not take any of her garbage seriously.

The following two squad members have less profile, Ayanna Pressley of Massachusetts and Rashida Talib of Michigan. Only Talib made a minor splash after her election to Congress, and I quote,

> *"Let us go to Washington and impeach the motherfucker."*

And that they did.

The political right is not much better. No solution to the fundamental problems is in the minds of our current set of politicians.

All "*bills*" are full of pork of any kind. It is only a few million here and there. Billions used to be the boundary, but now trillions are the size du jour.

Going from billion to trillion was easy and straightforward.
     Add only three more zeros to the existing nine.

Why didn't we think of that solution earlier?

On the lighter side, the German satirist Nuhr asked to define the difference between Republicans and Democrats; he responded there is none.

Why?

Democrats kill people before they are born, and Republicans use guns later!

Not too funny for dogmatic party members but amusing to pragmatic ones.

How do politicians do fiscally? It is a sad story that has no happy conclusion in sight.

Consecutive record federal tax revenues, 2013 to 2019, are insufficient to cover all federal expenditures, resulting in record deficits.
  For the moment, low interest rates are the saving feature.

When will that end?

FY 2019	$3.46 trillion (about $11,000 per person in the US) (actual)
FY 2018	$3.33 trillion (about $10,000 per person in the US)
FY 2017	$3.32 trillion
FY 2016	$3.27 trillion
FY 2015	$3.25 trillion
FY 2014	$3.02 trillion (about $9,300 per person in the US)
FY 2013	$2.77 trillion (about $8,500 per person in the US)

What can we say about politicians in general?

> *They love to spend someone else's money.*
> *They are unable to stay within record-level tax revenues.*
> *They never remove any expenditure, never mind how useless.*
> *They burden future generations with our current social payments.*
> *They only care about the millionaires' and billionaires' tax rates and give a hoot about maximizing total tax revenue.*
> *Punishing the rich is more important than controlling the national debt.*
> *Politicians of neither party have a workable structural answer.*

However, radicals knock on the door to dismantle the system while offering no practical, workable solution.

Notes:

_____

_____

_____

_____

_____

Mainstream Press

Gone are the days of Cronkite, Huntley, Brinkley, and others who simply reported the news. The commentary section held their opinions. The "*News*" was news, and "*Opinion*" was opinion.

The emergence of cable, a blessing for various general content, turned news reporting upside down.

The explosion of competing channels trans-formed news into opinion and, in the end, into biased political positions.
Ratings govern the reporting.

They are turning a little news flash into the story of the day.

The target is, get as many eyeballs as possible; never mind the distortion and manipulation of fact.

But all those opinion people still have press credentials, thus are members of the mainstream PRESS!

The Internet made the situation even worse. Now anybody can post anything on many social-media platforms. The term "*fake news*" appeared, rightfully so.

Who in that environment can discern fact from fiction?
Nobody!

Most news shows are propaganda channels for political parties, political interest groups, or, worse, a conduit for destructive forces. In the end, conspiracy theories veiled as fact and news.

Polls drive the daily news cycle—the motto du jour.

He who shouts the loudest and lies the best in the most convincing manner gets the most votes!

Lies are votes, votes are eyeballs, eyeballs are ratings, and ratings are MONEY!

Is that the modern way to send the news to the country?

Notes:

_____

_____

_____

_____

_____

Judiciary

Judiciary is the third pillar of government within the public sector. Sometimes it does not appear that way.

Here's a scene from a bad horror movie:

> *One of the Supremes is fighting countless battles against our archenemy, cancer. An international pharma conglomerate has found a mind-altering cancer treatment. It prolongs the life expectancy of the Supreme if she votes as told. The sinister pharma company drug can decelerate and accelerate cancer growth, depending on how the Supreme influences colleges on critical issues. The Supreme wants to stay alive until her party comes back to power. She wants to repay her party, no matter what!*
> *What does she do?*

Movies are movies, and reality is different!

Is it?

Justices at the Supreme Court, with their lifetime appointments while fighting countless personal illnesses at a very advanced age, do not strike a lot of confidence in anybody.

While the individual story is tragic, the overt impression and its consequences are not comforting.

Why do we have that situation?

Only the president can nominate Justices, while the Senate confirms. Formerly, nominees of either party received +90 percent votes. Now a simple majority will do.

Each party wants to get its ideology onto the court and get the court to vote along ideological lines.

Thus, liberal Justices "hang on for dear life" if conservatives are in charge and vice versa.

Who wins, and who loses?

The aging and sick Supremes stay in power while the country losses.

Who gains? The ideology in power that nominates the replacement!

Judges and Justices should be unbiased and guided by the law of the land. Yet they end up in 5 to 4 decisions in critical cases.

How can that be?

Any other scientific discipline, any problem, has only one "*optimum solution.*" There may be subsets of different practical solutions, but there is always only one "*optimum solution.*"

Not in law!

The legal profession thrives on a plurality of solutions, even at its highest level.

Lower courts run similarly.

Go to the West Coast, and one gets a vastly different decision from the ones made by East Coast courts.

Thus, politicians go "court shopping!"

Notes:

_____

_____

_____

_____

_____

Environment and Climate Change

The current emphasis on *"environmental and climate issues"* around the globe is a good thing. Governments of any country make grand plans to address the various issues.

Save the planet—the motto du jour.

Young people enthusiastically demonstrate their opposition to policies supported by their parents.

The time is now, and we have only XYZ time to "save the planet!"

Some of the problems in environmental areas are obvious and without dispute. Having islands of plastic drifting in our oceans is one of those. However, how to control the temperature rise of our planet is another problem altogether.

What indisputable facts do we have as indicators causing the temperature to rise? Without trying to go into the weeds of the problem, here are several facts cited by science:

The end of the last Little Ice Age was about 1850, and the planet resumed warming about then.

The measured receding of glaciers started on or around 1825–50.

The measured rise in our oceans of about seven inches per century started in or around 1860.

The extensive use of hydrocarbons in our industries started on or about the end of WWII.

Here is a simple question:

Given that man-made CO_2 emissions of our vast hydrocarbon use are the primary cause of global warming, what precipitated the onset of global warming in or about the 1825–60 period?

Anyone care to answer?

Notes:

_____

_____

_____

_____

_____

Growing Population

The world's population is currently near 7.5 billion, with the current growth adding another billion within twelve to fourteen years. Those numbers are vast and expanding.

In 1850–60, there were about 1.3 billion people globally.

Another factoid: Populations in developing countries seem to grow faster than in developed countries.

The globalists, demanding open borders every-where, advocate unrestricted mass migration, typically from south to north.

Siberia and northern Canada are the exception, too cold and no infrastructure.

What would such a policy do?

Virtually all developing nations—be it Africa, Middle East, South America, or Middle America—would be empty countries void of people!

Most importantly, prosperous receiving countries would become weak, mainly if such migration is uncontrolled over a brief period.

We can expect this to be valid for both Europe and the USA.

Deforestation of rain forests and forests, in general, is one of the top concerns. The same is true for any natural resource, except hydrocarbons, which environmentalists prefer to keep in the ground. However,

as long as the number of people expands, there is more demand for any resource, never mind what!

Notes:

_____

_____

_____

_____

_____

Technology

Technology is one of the key drivers of any modern economy. Unfortunately, poor or lack of education restricts people from equally taking part in the blessings. Modern-day life is hard to imagine without the use of technology. There are prominent examples such as phones, computers, TVs, the Internet, and the like, which help and hinder our daily lives.

Access to information is everything.

Social contacts without real contacts are one of the unfortunate consequences.

More in the background are those incredible advancements in medicine, artificial intelligence, and management of supply chains, which we all take for granted but act surprised when things go wrong.

That said, we, modern creatures of our society, cannot survive without our accustomed technology pieces.

Periodic, nonfunctioning infrastructure components are already early warning signals.

It does not take a genius to figure out that any technology's advancement is key to any nation's future survival.

Notes:

_____

_____

_____

_____

_____

National Defense

The US takes national defense very seriously and, by doing so, ended up being the world's police officers. It is part of the national pride, being the undisputed leader of the free world. Successes during the last one hundred years have led to that mindset.

The complexities of modern warfare create a regularly escalating cost, which the US cannot finance ad infinitum.

Creating a free Western Europe is the most significant accomplishment achieved during the period. But freeing millions of people living under communism in Eastern Europe is no small feat either, even though not a shot fired for that achievement.

Being the self-appointed policemen of the world created a problem of dependency everywhere in the world.

US forces live in Germany, Japan, and South Korea as guardians, even though those former enemies are now among the wealthiest nations and, top it off, very stable democracies.

Over the years, the former WWII ally Russia has become a thorn in the eye of US defense efforts. Even though Russia is not an economic power on equal footing with the US, its energy is directed continuously against the US.

Why are they so bold?

Answer!

Russia has a shitload of nukes! Those may be useless for most practical issues, but they are nukes nonetheless.

By the way, nukes are the most useless weapon systems for any country, yet they are the most dangerous weapon for any non-country entity.

The old "communism versus capitalism" mindset might be to blame. Russia is wary of Western invasions, which took place throughout its history. A paradigm change might be in order.

Strive for inclusion rather than exclusion.

The ramifications for both parties and Europe could be "priceless!"

Notes:

_____

_____

_____

_____

_____

International Relations

Economic interdependency and inclusion are the peacemakers du jour. The EU has brought peace to Europe. Historic wars among the various parties are outdated.

Former enemies France and Germany are now kissing cousins and, as a "fringe benefit," control the EU's affairs.

Great Britain did not like that, so they bailed out and left.

The facts are clear; mutual economic interdependency creates lasting peace.

With that in mind, it is hard to understand the exit of Great Brittan from the EU. Given all EU countries would think that way, the well-known "shit" would eventually hit the fan.

Hopefully, in the distant future, the EU can become the United States of Europe with all the benefits and obligations, and Great Britain decides to come back into the fold.

The US relationship with China is a difficult one at best.

China's ace in the sleeve is the vast economic market, exploited ruthlessly by getting Westerners to dance to their tune.

Greedy profit-driven corporations seem to forget that they deal with a communist dictatorship. Simultaneously, the communists have morphed into their form of capitalism, a type invented by them. And Western companies do just about anything to please the commies. And in the end, they lose most, if not all, their technological advantage.

Thus, all the capitalist corporations from all capitalist countries are swallowing the bait and the hock.

Hock, line, and sinker!

....

The Chinese have another edge, a long-term vision of where they want to be, say in ten, twenty, thirty, forty, fifty years.

....

And this is a significant advantage over fragmented acting individual corporations.

....

Aside from that, they do what they must do to succeed: steal, intimidate, manipulate, and export all their products to the West.

....

Let the West finance the transformation from an agricultural-based society to a high-tech one.

And it seems to work.

Western corporations, trying to perfect their supply chains by reducing costs to the bare minimum, created a total dependency on China. The COVID-19 pandemic proved that minimum expenses are only one part, but not the most significant one. They learned the hard way:

You cannot get the stuff when you need it the most.

The Chinese are willing to gamble whenever it suits them, e.g., support North Korea's nuclearization as long as all the missiles point to Los Angeles and not Beijing. The Chinese motto: Keep the US occupied with trying to denuclearize North Korea.

....

There is no surprise there; China wants to surpass the United States in any aspect possible, and they are using any method possible.

....

The Chinese dictatorship does not tolerate any dissent! For example, Hong Kong endured peaceful or not-so-peaceful protests over two years. Initially, Chinese troops assembled near the border, and nothing happened.

Then they deployed a democratic solution to the problem and created a law specifically for Hong Kong.

All dissenters will have to face the mainland China court system, which typically deals out harsh and long sentences for such offenses. *Problem solved!*

The Chinese population is not monolithic, far from it! Minorities who want to preserve and keep their language, religion, and cultural identity face transfer into reeducation camps. We have seen those practices before. Does Nazi Germany ring a bell?

Dictatorships strive for a homogeneous population; differences are not welcome there.

The military buildup on artificial islands in the South China Sea challenges maritime law and neighboring countries. Protests are abundant, but nothing happens. Except the Chinese continue to expand and strengthen their islands.

The United States is wary of wars, and the Chinese know it.

And nobody besides the United States can mount a challenge!

The Middle East is and has been a powder keg for the last two millennia. And today is not any different, even more so.

Formerly, the region was the cradle of civilization, while now it is a supplier of oil, misery, and brutal religious extremists.

While they hate each other for one reason or another, they generally unite in hating all Western-origin people, the Crusaders!

The Crusades happened from around 1095 to 1492. Christians were fighting Muslims to free the Holy Land.

So conceptually, nothing has changed in the last 700 to 1,200 years! Except some of the extreme religious lunatics want to go back to that period!

It seems that all Western efforts to help that region fail as the term "Crusaders" tends to unite them in hatred toward the West.

Historically, Afghanistan was the gateway to Asia in its glory days. Those days are gone. Its tribal structure, weak or nonexistent education, and adherence to a literal interpretation of the Quran make it what it is, an uncivilized throwback to the Dark Ages. Its primary exports are opium and Islamic terrorism, none of those products are desirable from a Western perspective. It is also the place of the most prolonged American war engagement, with no end in sight.

So why are the United States and its allies still there?

Is it pride?
The Soviets had to leave with their tail between their legs, and now, all Western forces may need to do likewise?

Not a pretty picture!
The United States should have taken the Vietnam lesson to heart.

You cannot beat an ideology, be it communism or Islam, with military means!

It was financial means then, but now religion unites the enemy. It follows that only a change in the religious reward system will bring about change.

The African continent is known as the Dark Continent. It stands for an intriguing place to visit for Westerners. Historical tribal living is exciting to see from a visitor's perspective. Still, it does not solicit the same response from the locals, who must endure the hardships of primitive living and the associated poverty.

There are two primary sources of income for the continent: tourism and valuable natural resources. Those two industries are insufficient to increase living standards, principally if corruption and warfare impede all progress. On top of it, the populations in the various countries virtually explode.

Thus, Africa is poised to be an enormous threat of massive migration of biblical proportions to Europe absent a domestic solution. Measures to contain have thus far failed to solve the problem. Thousands of migrants perish annually, trying to escape poverty via the Mediterranean Sea route.

The migrants see the promised land in the north, and they will continue to come if poverty, warfare, and corruption overwhelm their respective countries.

They have nothing to lose!

South and Middle America are analogous cases to Africa. In many cases, tourism is the only practical industry for some countries. Others are much more sophisticated, have more diverse sources of income, yet adhere to profoundly rooted corruption. Others have vast amounts of precious natural resources, yet, led by incompetent or corrupt politicians adhering to a nonfunctioning political philosophy, do nothing but fail! Others have gangs virtually running the country!

You name it, and they got it!

Again, poverty and the desire for safety becomes a driver and motivator for people to migrate north to the promised land, the wealthiest country in the world, the USA.

Unfortunately, many of the home-cooked problems migrate with the migrants. Gangs move via the migration route and expand their enterprise on a larger scale.

Selling drugs is what gangs do best.

Notes:

_____

_____

_____

_____

_____

What Can We Deduce from the Preceding?

Let us start with the most critical deduction.

> **We have massive yet-to-be-solved problems.**
> **And, oh yeah, few or NO solutions on the horizon.**

It is evident that politicians, particularly career ones, are not part of the solution; they are part of the problem.

And then we find the pleasant exception, the Trump presidency.

We have a novice politician—a billionaire who knew only two colors, black or white, and seemingly hated gray and was hated or loved by half of the country.

> **And even more odd, he connected with the ordinary folks yet was despised by the snobs, academia, pseudo-intellectuals and intellectuals, most of Hollywood, "mainstream press," and the entire Left Coast.**

Oh, let us not forget the bureaucrats; there was no love there.

> **That is why he was an enigma wrapped in a riddle!**

As for concrete policies, he failed with Kim Jong-Un, the North Korean dictator, but got a deal with Xi Jinping, the Chinese dictator. *So he is one and one with dictators!*

The "Chinese virus" COVID-19 turned out to be Trump's most significant success not only for the nation but for the entire world.

> *Even though Trump defeated COVID-19, paradoxically, the virus defeated Trump!*

Trump was lukewarm about managing the virus, and people did not get comfort from that behavior.

> *You cannot be lukewarm as a politician—disingenuous, yes, but under no circumstances, lukewarm!*

Enough said about the exception, and back to our "trustworthy" politicians.

> *If record tax revenues are insufficient, we must find other ways and means to solve structural issues.*

Most politicians have a deficiency in their vocabulary; the term "wealth creation" is missing.

> *Unfortunately, they are too well acquainted with wealth distribution.*

President John F. Kennedy once made a profound statement:

> *"Ask not what the country can do for you; ask what you can do for the country!"*

That statement is needed now, more than ever, to address virtually all the issues that require resolutions.

....

It was right then and is true now.

....

Oh yeah, we got too many symptoms to choose to diagnose our underlying problems and identify the needed permanent solutions.

But do we?

Any medical doctor would be delighted to find that many symptoms!

What we have are a physician's dream and a patient's nightmare.

And we, the nation, are the patients.

Common sense tells us that jumping to solutions at this point would not solve anything. Without more information, we would put only Band-Aids on broken bones and gaping wounds.

Let us look at "paradoxes"; they are plentiful throughout our economic, political, and international structures. Maybe that approach gets us away from thinking like everybody else and opens our eyes to new and different solutions.

Notes:

_____

_____

_____

_____

_____

LET US CONSIDER A FEW PARADOXES

Looking around, each one of us can name the two biggest paradoxes within our society. Let me suggest my top two!

Currently, the US cannot fulfill its social obligation without incurring a sizeable ongoing budget deficit that accumulates a debt in astronomical numbers. Now what is the paradox, you might want to ask?

Paradox # 1: While the US federal government collects the highest total tax receipts in its history, its expenditures on social payments such as Medicare, Medicaid, and Social Security and its expenditures on national security far exceed its intakes. Consequently, while trying to be socially responsible toward its currently living citizens, the nation is burdening its future citizens for many generations to come.

This behavior of our current set of politicians in power proves that present votes are more valuable than future ones.

It is a safe bet that the future generation will not judge us kindly.

Paradox #2: The wealthiest nation in the world, crushed by its social obligations, faces the stigma of being not very social at all.

A sizable percentage of its population wants to increase social "investments" to correct this perception.

With that introduction, let us examine several existing paradoxes. The presented list is not exclusive; however, they all have a common denominator: They affect the private sector's functioning.

Notes:

_____

_____

_____

_____

_____

World Peace Paradox

"The more we reduce weapons of war, the higher the chance of having a conflict" paradox.

Or…

"The weaker the United States Military, the higher the chance of creating a stronger European Union Military" paradox.

Why do we have such a paradox? Answer: Some people believe that disarmament is the solution, while many others think peace through strength.

Let us start with an unusual "Pope Speech."

Pope Francis on ISIS in March 2015: He urged "everyone, in line with their possibilities, (to) act to alleviate the suffering" of those currently being persecuted by ISIS and assured those targeted by the terrorists that they "have not been forgotten."

Translating "Pope-speak": He asks for military intervention; otherwise, he would call for nonviolent means.

So even the Pope recognizes that "peace" is hard to come by and prayers may be insufficient to solve a problem promptly.

Pope aside, what does it mean, "world peace"?
No war?

No small scrimmages?
Or better yet, everybody loves everybody.
While we are at it, for how long?

Humanity never managed to be entirely at peace. At least during my lifetime, world peace did not occur. Thus far, one can always dream, can't we?

And a dream it is!

To reach that state, some enlightened people call for arms reduction.

Really?

Let me remind everyone of the 1994 local conflict in Rwanda. The Hutus and Tutsi did not like each other very much but did not have modern weapons as guns, cannons, tanks, and the like. They had knives, machetes, and baseball bat-like objects. Using those primitive weapons, they managed to kill 800,000 people (about South Dakota's population) in a mere one hundred days!

Looking at some big wars fought during my lifetime, say Vietnam. That war used just about every modern warfare tool, except nukes, and resulted in a US fatality level of 58,220 over eleven years.

A sarcastic observer would conclude that you don't need modern tools to get the job done, which is false, of course!

The moral of that story is, disarmament does not do the trick alone.

Unfortunately, there are too many examples of hate-driven atrocities committed in our modern, enlightened time.

Thus, the sad conclusion.

World peace may be the biggest illusion of humanity!

Humans resolve conflicts through war, and wars require killing, killing intended to stop the fighting. Which, in turn, always opens fresh wounds and creates unknown reasons for having another war.

A few "**maybe**" options

....

Maybe "paradox" is wrong, and its proper title is "world peace illusion"!

Maybe we need to define the mission of any Western armed force in the following terms:

- *Defend its territory.*
- *Act as a deterrent.*
- *Supply fast response or help for natural disasters.*
- *Eliminate any dictator, tyrant, or religious fanatic that indiscriminately kills people and threatens any common-good interests.*

Maybe the intuitive solution "*No weapons, no war*" does not apply to humanity. Humanity, throughout its existence, was engaged in violence. Pacifist nations like Japan must rethink their military-use stance as the world still is a violent and dangerous place.

Maybe we need to tell the EU that it needs to be capable of protecting the European theater, thereby forcing the EU to form a European Army capable of defending itself against bullies like Vladimir Putin.

Such a solution would strengthen the defense expenditures overall but significantly reduce the US share.

Maybe for the EU, there is a way to encourage it to quit free-loading off the USA expenditures for national security.

The time for a free ride is over.

Maybe we need to tell the EU that US military forces leave the European theater in a timetable consistent with EU forces' buildup.

Maybe we want to reduce the US military budget at the rate of EU buildup. In the end, the joint forces should be greater than the US forces' size at any point in time.

Maybe a system of "**inclusion**," instead of "**exclusion**," should be the dominant concept assuring world peace.

"Trust, but verify." President Ronald Reagan.

Maybe we ought to encourage the EU to consider the **inclusion** of Russia into the EU. Having Russia as a partner will contribute to more openness and forestall surprises.

Maybe the **inclusion** of Russia into NATO will take away the justified fear of Russians. While Vladimir Putin must justify his aggression toward its former Western-leaning Soviet satellite countries, Russia might become a real democracy.

Maybe Vladimir Putin will give the EU plenty of encouragement to fork out more money for its national defense. It is astonishing to see that a $3 trillion GDP dwarf can threaten an $18 trillion giant, and the said giant still is virtually defenseless.

It is clear.
Nukes talk louder than words!

Being a mighty pacifist does duly impress the world's intellectuals but does not stop a pragmatic bully.

Maybe there is an interaction of social and military expenditures, as shown in the mass exodus of desperate people fleeing from poverty and war in the Middle East and Central Africa. Solving local problems in those regions will prevent future social issues and refugee explosions in Europe.

Emptying those regions cannot be in the best interest of anybody!

Maybe the private sector should reconsider trying to make every nickel and dime in China.

Notes:

_____

_____

_____

_____

_____

High Government Spending Paradox

"The more money we borrow for current social programs, the smaller the size of available funds for future generations' social efforts" paradox.

Or...

"The stealing money from your children" paradox.

The genesis of this paradox is the desire to do good now. On the one hand, we have people who want to be socially just now, never mind the insufficient funds. And on the other hand, we have the same number of people who wish to have national security be the policemen of the world!

So we satisfy both by spending lots of money we do not have.

Have you ever seen government action that reduces expenditure? No! Politicians like to show compassion, and politically motivated compassion requires money, lots of money, particularly money we currently do not have. So we borrow to the hilt.

Simple problem, simple solution!

Most politicians do recognize that there is a problem, while some do not. Those who do not resort to creative language hide the painful truth. They call all those questionable expenditures *"investments."* For example, only politicians refer to current social payments as investments and, astonishingly enough, can support their action through *"intellectual gymnastics"* provided by their *"think tanks."* The product of such mental exercise is appropriately named *"Washington speak."*

Unfortunately, "Washington speak" does not solve the problem; it merely hides it and helps to accelerate the unfortunate situation.

A few "**maybe**" options

Maybe we ought to quit spending our future generation's money on our social well-being and national security and try to live within our means.

Maybe printing money to fund our budget deficit will create future inflation. It is certainly not a question of *if*, it is only a question of *when*.

Maybe having no plan to end government budget deficits and pay off the debt is an unsocial act toward future generations and a paradox in itself.

Having a social conscience for our current generation and being socially irresponsible toward future generations certainly is a paradox.

Notes:

_____

_____

_____

_____

_____

Illegal Immigration Paradox

"The more we promote the virtues, advantages, and riches of our democratic societies, the more people will try to participate either legally or illegally" paradox.

Or…

"We also want to share in your great fortune" paradox.

Illegal immigration, migration, or being a refugee are at the center of this paradox. In Europe or the US, Western democracies promote their high standard of living everywhere globally through modern media. Thus, it becomes a magnet for all those desperate people.

And come, they do!

Surprise, surprise, on the respective borders, instead of open arms, they find closed doors.

Here might be an excellent place to talk about the German "*Wirtschaftswunder.*"

What is that, you might ask?

Concisely, a reference to the absolute astonishing economic recovery of West Germany from the overwhelming destruction of World War II. The catalyst for this recovery was the US Marshall Plan. Which, in retrospect, turned out to be one of the boldest investments the US ever made.

But that is not the story!

The story is about what happened after that. Rebuilding the country's infrastructure and economy required labor, lots of labor West Germany did not have. So the state created the "*Gastarbeiter Program.*" The "*Guest Worker Program*" was also the catalyst for a faster economic recovery for all the source countries: Italy, Spain, the former Yugoslavia, Greece, and Turkey.

Now how does this reference help to solve the underlying illegal immigration problem?

Simple, a booming economy requires lots of labor the US does not have.

Issuing "*guest worker visas*" generously will help the US and the source countries, just as in the West German example.

A few "**maybe**" options

Maybe we can switch our problem-solving approach from "*exclusion*" to "*inclusion*." Certainly, exclusion has only created a climate of fear and "*underground living*" among the "*illegals*."

Maybe we ought to give all "*illegal immigrants*" work permits at the border, document their entry, and make them legal. Giving them legal status will make them taxpayers and allow them to become part of society. Those who cannot find a job will return to their home countries on their own.

Maybe building a "*fence*" is not the highest priority.

Maybe we ought to learn from the lesson of the "*Prohibition Period*." Making alcohol illegal did not end drinking; it just created American royalty, aka "the *Kennedys* and Al Capone."

Maybe we ought to punish job providers of "*undocumented workers*" with severe fines to end those poor souls' existing abuse.

Maybe a path to US citizenship is only possible after twenty to thirty years for people with illegal entry, while legal entrants can do so after five years.

Maybe we can convince unions that those workers are not a threat to their jobs while growing the economy at a 3–4 percent rate.

Maybe our aging population needs "*guest workers*" for our economy to function in support of our existing social obligations.

Maybe we ought to look at the current European refugee problem and envisage such an occurrence for the western hemisphere. Wars and the emergence of dictators are not unheard of in Middle and South America. We can help stabilize that region by giving jobs to desperate people while increasing their home countries' prosperity.

Maybe we ought to listen to Albert Einstein.

---

*"**Insanity: Doing the same thing over and over again and expecting a different outcome.**"*

Notes:

_____

_____

_____

_____

_____

Two Parties' Political Landscape Paradox

"Two parties will always find a compromise"
paradox.

Or…

"The more we argue, debate, and obstruct, the
better the solution and progress" paradox.

The two-party system should not have the paradox we have now.

Not too long ago, the US two-party system was
the envy of the world.

The parties worked together in tough and trying times and fought out their differences when time permitted.

Those were the good old days, even back to 9/11.

No more!

Dogmatic posturing replaced practical problem-solving.

What happened?

The Reps and the Dems drifted philosophically apart, and the new leadership was unable even to consider a compromise; affright, it might upset either end of the membership spectrum. The new mantra, "the party first and the country second," is embedded in each party platform. And what is even more disturbing, no effort is on the horizon to reverse course!

Politicians became more daring in distorted political speech. Outright lies with trustworthy eyes in front of TV cameras are the norm and no longer the exception. All done with the assumption that all listeners and viewers are stupid and unable to see the charade.

The uncrowned king of such presentations is, without any doubt, "Shifty Schiff."

So the gap is widening until all civility is gone.

What comes next?

A few "**maybe**" options

Maybe we ought to consider the formation of a third party to end the Washington political two-party stalemate. And solve some big problems like a perpetual budget deficit!

An issue-based third party can be the problem solver.

Maybe we can create a home for the Independent voter!

Maybe the Independent voter can finally become genuinely independent.

Switch from being screwed by both parties to being the screwier, only if necessary!

Maybe the existence of a third party will bring both established parties back to their original mission.

Conduct the people's business.

Maybe a third party can change Washington's sole focus on power struggles to an exclusive focus on shared solutions.

Maybe a third party can change Washington to live within its means and implement debt-reduction measures.

Wouldn't it be nice if our legislators tried to reduce the budget deficit and reversed the debt accumulation?

Notes:

_____

_____

_____

_____

Education Paradox

"The more illiterate and dysfunctional people we create at the low end of our education system, the higher the prison population" paradox.

Or...

"The pay me now or pay me later" paradox.

Or...

"Still illiterate after twelve years of schooling" paradox.

We live in a country of extremes! The rich get richer, and the poor get poorer. Money-wise, yes, but education-wise?

The rich get more competent, and the poor get more illiterate, dumber?

How can that be?

On the upper end, we have an education system for people with money that is second to none worldwide.

And on the other extreme, it can be merely shameful. Thus, the paradox.

People worldwide stand in line to be part of the outstanding institutions of higher learning, whether student or teacher; it does not matter.

It is the allure of innovative research for the teacher and the student's magic certificate that opens all doors. They all have a motive and are well rewarded.

But what about the other end of the spectrum?

We have run-down inner-city schools that teach nothing worthwhile. Proficient reading and writing are optional, and job prospects are nonexistent. Teachers' unions block any student from going to a better school, a school of choice for the poor souls who want to learn something useful for the future!

Their reward?

> ***They have outstanding prospects of a life of crime with a high likelihood of graduating to prison.***

And that vicious cycle repeats itself generation after generation. So we must ask ourselves: Can we, as a society, live in such an awful situation?

The clear answer should be NO; we should do something about it.

A few "**maybe**" options

Maybe we can close failing schools and begin from scratch.

Maybe we can look at failing teachers as well?

Maybe we can look at teacher unions and demand higher standards within a given time!

Maybe we can segregate students based on their academic aptitude.

Maybe we can move all failing students to boarding schools.

It works for the rich. Why not try it for the poor?

Maybe we can give teachers the power to remove any student from their class who does not conform to rules.

Make attending schools a privilege, not a right.

Notes:

_____

_____

_____

_____

_____

Free Society Paradox

"Maximum freedom also means accepting the unproductive part of that society" paradox.

Or...

"The support your local bum" paradox.

The use of freedom is at the core of this paradox. Not all actions by a free society are desirable. People can do stupid, unproductive things in a free society. Hopefully, those are significantly less than all the productive ones.

The US society is, without question, the most accessible society ever assembled throughout human history.

It is a bunch of big words that could not be truer. People from about any corner of the world came to this country to be part of it. We typically refer to it as the melting pot.

The term implies mingling, combining, or absorbing, all words that suppose a gradual loss of national, racial, or religious identity over time.

We have a natural process that leads to a highly diverse American individual.

All of that being a good thing. It is also clear that some of those traits are favorable and some are not.

What does all that have to do with a free society?

All those presumably negative traits could lead to unfortunate expressions in a free society, not equally favored by everyone.
But it is shared nonetheless.

And to be able to do so makes it a free society.

A few **maybe** options

Maybe not all persons living in a free society can enjoy all freedoms.

Sort out privileges and entitlements.

Maybe maximizing freedom must also mean maximizing the productive part of society.

Maybe people making unwise choices such as drug abuse, forgoing mandatory education requirements, forever being a burden to society as a matter of choice, and the like must lose some of their freedom in the form of compulsory reeducation and training.

Notes:

_____

_____

_____

_____

_____

Race Inequality Paradox

"The more we accuse each other of being racists, the easier it is to solve the race problem" paradox

Or…

"Anybody who is White, enjoying White privileges, must be a racist" paradox.

Unfortunately, racial inequality is one of the stains in US history.

History's burden is what it is, and none of today's revisionary efforts will wipe it away.

At the outset, the problem was slavery, then it became discrimination, and now it is what?

A clear statement of the problem will yield viable solutions, while race-baiting rhetoric will do nothing but open the divide.

So what is the root cause of today and not yesterday's problem? The problem is not the history of slavery and discrimination, and any efforts to rewrite it will not solve the problem.

We have a group of people who go to the worst schools in the nation, live in astonishing poor neighborhoods riddled with crime, and have no prospects for supporting themselves and their families.

Now what could go wrong with that scenario?

A few **maybe** options

....

Maybe we ought to suggest, encourage, or, god forbid, enforce mixed-race marriages. In a few generations, no White or Black race will exist, only a gray one.

Doing any of those actions will end the "race problem" after a few generations. Everybody becomes Black and White and yellow!

Even the genetically inclined racists!

Maybe we ought to shut down our failing schools at inner cities and build new ones that produce students who, in the end, know helpful stuff.

Maybe we ought to renovate our inner cities and create job prospects for our educated students.

Maybe we want to encourage two-parent families and not discourage them.

Maybe we want to expand the job prospects for inner-city kids beyond drugs and gangs.

Maybe we ought to disinvite the profiteering race hater, Al Sharpton, from future funerals.

Al does not seem to want to solve the race-inequality problem.

He wants to profit from them!

Maybe Al does not want to solve the race inequality problem, but we all should.

Notes:

_____

_____

_____

_____

_____

Law and Order Paradox

....

> **"The more we attack our police, the higher the crime rate" paradox.**

....

Or…

> *"The more we defund the police, the more we encourage our criminals" paradox.*

Or…

> *"The more we say we help poor neighborhoods by reducing the police, the more they suffer from unrestrained criminals" paradox.*

Or…

> *"The more we remove guns from law-abiding citizens, the higher the use of firearms by criminals" paradox.*

We certainly face a paradox of wanting police protection while, at the same time, distrusting the power and authority of the police.

> ***The US has done an excellent job being the policeman of the world on a macroscale.***

Millions of people received the privilege of freedom all around the world.

And yet, even there, the US is criticized by some of the recipients on nonessential grounds.

Maybe, just maybe, it is about expecting perfection from the overly generous "Uncle Sam."

> ***On the microscale, the US police have a questionable racial bias history.***

May I utter the word Selma, Al?

Thus, it is not too surprising that there is a distrust among the Black population toward the police.

The problem is not a one-sided issue; disenfranchised Black youth disrespect the law with an in-your-face attitude, leading to unfortunate physical confrontations with no winners and only losers.

Occasionally, we have a dead police officer, which gets only token press coverage. And in not-too-frequent intervals, we have the unfortunate outcome of a Black person killed by a police officer—all of it documented by the entire cadre of bystanders via video recording. All of it despicable but preventable.

What comes next?

An earthshaking explosion that blows up the entire nation via protests, riots, and the required looting. For what?

Unfortunately, that process will continue to repeat itself if we do not answer the problem's root cause.

A few **maybe** options

Maybe we all should support our law-enforcement personnel. We surely need them in times of crisis.

There are bad apples in any profession; we have laws to correct any problems.

Society at large seems to retaliate by killing about a hundred of them every year.

Now who in his right mind wants that job?

Maybe we should cut the police some slack.

Putting their ass on the line for a miserable few thousand dollars a year, anyone could go "postal."

Maybe we should recognize 99 percent of good once every year for a job well done.

Maybe we ought to consider reducing the police force after we see a decline in wrongdoing.

Getting criminals, white- or blue-collar, to swear on a stack of Bibles might work?

Notes:

_____

_____

_____

_____

_____

Social Compassion or Wealth Distribution Paradox

"The more we spend on 'social programs,' the more we increase social inequality" paradox.

Or…

"The more we redistribute money from the more fortunate to less fortunate people, the longer it takes to decrease the less fortunate population. Even worse, the more we redistribute wealth, the more we increase the dependent population" paradox.

Or…

We could also call it the "how to maintain your poverty" paradox.

Or…

"The more we spend on 'social programs' today, the happier our grandkids" paradox.

Or…

"The more we borrow today, the more grateful our future generations" paradox.

The wealth distribution paradox here is not the typical one we all think of when asked.

No, it is the one from one generation to another and another and another.

> ***Thus, what we spend and borrow, our grand-children will pay and pay again.***

Cruel, isn't it?

And what is *social* now turns *asocial* in the future. Do we want to behave that way?

> ***Socially compassionate people say no; progres-sives say yes.***

Who is wrong, and who is right?

Hopefully, this book, with your help, will supply some answers and solutions.

A few **maybe** options

Maybe burdening our future generations with our current social expenditures is not such a brilliant idea.

Maybe such behavior should be more appropriately labeled "stealing from future generations."

*Stealing from yet-to-be-born generations is most likely "the most **asocial** behavior known to humanity."*

Nobody should condone such behavior!

Maybe the **most social** behavior known to humanity is "giving a person a self-sustaining job!"

Giving a person a self-sustaining job allows any person to become a productive member of society. It converts dependents or burdens into contributors.

More importantly, maximizing the number of contributors will reduce the social burden of society to a minimum.

Maybe we should cherish our job creators. They are the cornerstone of our society.

Maybe we ought to rethink our policies to solve social-inequality problems with money.

The war on poverty programs spent $20 trillion over fifty years and reduced the poverty rate by 1 percent.

Maybe our rich-people deficit and poor-people surplus needs to be reversed.

Strive for a surplus of rich people and a deficit of poor people, and all the ills of society will disappear.

Maybe we need to keep some poor people for the protesters to protest, the mob to riot, the social engineers to social-engineer, the politician to save, the government bureaucrats to care for, and proof that we are not perfect, not yet anyway!

Maybe we should completely extract inner-city kids or rural kids from their destructive environment and send them to boarding schools for all their schooling.

We know this approach works for rich kids!

Can we do likewise by educating our society's weak strata and filling higher education institutions such as Harvard or Clemson with future leaders?

Contrast this with our current approach of filling USP's Florence ADX or Leavenworth or any other local jail with their future inmates.

We can teach those who do not have the aptitude for higher learning world-class skills while shamelessly copy from the German apprentice system.

Maybe we ought to reconsider the *"notion of a free society"* and ask ourselves.

How can we take the poor kids, put them in a first-class boarding school, and teach them knowledge and skills useful for their future while becoming contributing members of our free society?

How can we do this without the objections of our current crop of progressive social engineers?

We can expect race-division promoters like Al Sharpton, Jesse Jackson, and the like to call for riots.

We also should not expect any warm embraces from the teacher's unions of our failing schools.

Maybe education without jobs and opportunity are a no-no. Otherwise, we copy Fidel Castro's Cuba, and we all know how this has turned out over the last fifty years.

Maybe our newly minted workforce will allow companies to create and produce products exportable worldwide, like the German economy that has kept an export surplus since WWII.

We can reward companies and businesses for creating and keeping jobs.

Maybe we can make a public policy that rewards job creators and not stigmatize them.

> *"Giving a person a job is the most beneficial social contribution anyone can make, and our policies have to reflect that."*

Notes:

_____

_____

_____

_____

_____

Unbiased Judiciary Paradox

> *"Justice is blind, okay, but liberal or conservative?" paradox.*

Or…

"If you get sentenced in the WEST, go for appeal in the EAST and vice versa" paradox.

Or…

"Want a liberal Supreme Court? Support a liberal senator. Want a conservative Supreme Court? Support a conservative senator! Want a blind justice? Go to the School for the Blind" paradox.

An unbiased judiciary should not be a paradox, but it is these days. What is impartial about a conservative or liberal judge? The bias is right there in the open, carried as a proud label.

The judiciary is supposed to interpret the law and not make it; that is called separation of power.

The liberal faction thinks that they know more about the law than the ignorant lawmakers.

So we must deal with the superior-intelligence argument. Whatever it is, the judges are only nominated and confirmed, while the lawmakers are chosen and represent the people's will. Granted, lawmakers' lease on life in political terms is only two, four, six years, while judges enjoy a lifetime appointment.

One more thing, any judge who wants to make law should run for office and become a legislator!

What wrong with that?
Let's look at it from a judge's perspective!
For one, *"I am having all the innovative proposals scrutinized by all other ignorant legislators!"*

And second, *"I must get a vote to pass a particular piece of law."*

None of that happened in my chambers; there, I was the sole judge.

A few **maybe** options

....

Maybe we want a Supreme Court that issues, as a practice, 9 to 0 rulings. Only in exceptional cases, a descending vote is possible.

Maybe we want the best judges and not the best race, gender, ideology, or any other mix.

Maybe we want our Supremes or any other judge not to be older than seventy.

Even Supremes are not immune to mental and physical decline!

Maybe we do not want any judge to affiliate with any party.

Judges or Justices, by definition, are neutral.

Maybe the Senate must confirm any Justice or judge by greater than 90 percent.

Maybe ideology, liberal or conservative, becomes outdated in our judiciary.

Being called either liberal or conservative should be considered an insult to any judge or Justice!

Notes:

_____

_____

_____

_____

_____

The Politically Correct Society Paradox

....

"The politically correct (PC) or incorrect society" paradox.

....

What is PC, and why do we encounter it everywhere in our society? Most people seem to hate it, and only a few, the PC police, relish it.

Maybe stepping back in time will help.

Say fifty years ago, there was no such thing as being PC. All the issues we object to today were nonissues then, at least for most people.

What changed?

A whole lot of things changed quite significantly.

The draft compelled young men to join the military to fight and sometimes die for freedom.

The male members of most households brought in the money, while women stayed at home.

Black Americans faced open discrimination.

Gays and lesbians remained in the closet.

Those factors and other factors leave only one conclusion: We had a White male-dominated heterosexual society!

What do we have today?

The lesbians and gays left their closets, and all other forms of sexual endeavor joined the fray.

We formed a rainbow coalition with big parades.

Nothing is hidden, all in the open, and even the most conservative institution, the military, opened its doors in welcoming the new reality.

We revamped the military, no more draft and all men in the firing line; it is voluntary now!

We welcome everyone to shoot or get shot; we do not discriminate any longer.

We accept men, women, gays, lesbians, even gender neutrals, and all the other remaining segments of our society.

So that is quite different!

For Blacks, all open discriminations ended while still being at the bottom of the economic scale.

So parity is still miles away.

Improvements, yes, but satisfaction, no!

At home, the man is not the sole provider for most families any longer. We have homebound dads and working women in a 180-degree reversal. Yet it's both man and wife who have to work to make ends meet for most families. And while we are at it, we question the remnants of White male dominance every day.

How, you might ask?

First, in our language, many formerly acceptable, sometimes raunchy terms are not permitted any longer. And there are many of those. Humor about sex, race, religion, and national origin is strictly forbidden.

We became stale, bland, and cautious to please the PC crowd.

Taking a position on anything is only for the daring nonconformists, a dying rare breed!

We became a nation of a humorless and spineless conformist.

Second, before initiating actions, practices, and policies, we check its political correctness to be safe. Anything White and male is indeed a White-male privilege and, as such, not acceptable any longer. With all that...

The majority has become the perceived minority!

No one can argue against most of those changes. The question here are the following:

Where does it end?
And where is the boundary?
Has the pendulum swung too far?

We know that some changes were necessary; that is not the issue. The issue here are the changes, for change's sake! Like revising history and damaging and destroying any remembrance thereof! Or, even better, striving toward an egalitarian society in areas such as education, sports, business, and any other item of interest to you.

That cannot be good!

Now what did all that adherence to "political correctness" give us?

A better society?

One that is more productive, peaceful, dynamic, cohesive, or any other attribute you might find critical?

Quite the opposite; the more we yield to PC, the higher demand for more PC.

So it is like slime in a horror movie, all-consuming with relentless expansion and no end in sight.

A few **maybe** options

Maybe we ought to get our legislators to create laws for PC conformance. Ought!

Maybe we ought to create competitions for the highest PC conformance. Ought!

Maybe we ought to reward the most complying PC student and teachers. Ought!

Maybe we ought to create a new field of study, PC compliance, in every university. Ought!

Maybe we ought to just concentrate on fixing the underlying problems and do away with PC.

Notes:

_____

_____

_____

_____

_____

The Free Election Paradox

"The more people that participate and vote, the better and more accurate the election outcome" paradox.

Or…

"The more convenient the voting process, the fewer people will cheat the election process" paradox.

Or…

"The more controlled the voting process, the more unreliable and unjust the outcome" paradox.

Voting and its process are at the core of any democratic society. Why is it so important?

The voting public, in its aggregate, transfers the power of the people to the governing bodies.

That's why voting, the task, and the associated process must be beyond approach. Yet in the last two presidential elections, our nation did not fulfill that standard.

And there is another issue to consider.

The process of voting is the foundation, the bedrock for our functioning democratic society.

We, the voters, empower our elected leaders to act on our behalf.

That transfer of power from legitimate voters to elected leaders must instill confidence in voters across the entire spectrum regardless of political persuasion.

That did not happen in the last election!

Our 2020 elections set several new records even though we endured the restrictions of a pandemic.

Let's revisit some of the most impressive records.

The winner, President-elect Biden, received more than 81 million votes.

The loser, President Trump, amassed 74 million votes, both surpassing President Obama's record of 69 million votes.

Hum, an election process performed under severe restriction led to a voter-participation record!

Not by a little bit but by a lot!

Interesting!

So we set new participation records. For that to happen, a real significant process change had to take place.

You guessed it, "mail-in voting."

How did it happen?

Leisurely, all states opened the "spigot" for mail-in voting.

Every registered voter got a mail-in voter application.

Millions of voters mailed their votes.

That's how!

Everyone should be pleased with the successful outcome. Millions of voters participated in a pandemic.

Success is at hand!

Case closed!

Or did we open "Pandora's box"?

Trump cried foul, but the courts disagreed.

Trump won the "in-person" votes.
Biden won the "mail-in" votes.

Again, the case closed.

Let us look at the actual voting process to get a feel for what is right and what is wrong with expanding the voting process.

Let's look at the in-person voting process.

First, we try to verify the voter with a picture ID to ascertain the voter identity.

Now we know WHO is casting a vote.

Second, we cast a vote as a solitary, unencumbered action.

Now we know that nobody influenced the voter in casting their vote.

We see the voter did it and nobody else. Our system has safeguards to ensure an unencumbered voting process. Typically, we do not permit campaigning near the voting places

Thus, we know HOW!

Now let us look at the mail-in voting process. Right off the bat, we find a problem.

The two critical conditions of the in-person process—WHO and HOW—cannot be 100 percent assured with the mail-in vote.

We don't know for sure who cast a vote!
And we don't know who influenced the voter while casting a vote!

What we have is a definite maybe!

However, we know for sure we have an incredibly flawed process, and the political outcry is evidence of it.

Besides having a flawed process, we have an even more significant issue with the underlying philosophy of
"Who should be part of the voting public?"

**The traditionalists and the current law say,
*"Only registered citizens can vote!"***

The progressive view is quite different.

All adult residents should vote, including prisoners, illegal aliens, felons, legal residents, and the like.
Better stated, anybody older than seventeen, eighteen years old. Why stop there?

There is no common ground between those philosophies. And the turmoil after the last election is ample evidence of it.

One side believes that the voting process is an in-person activity, while the other side prefers no restrictions.

If that is not enough, there is another structural issue to consider. Namely, in any recent presidential election, there is this thing, the so-called swing states. Interestingly enough, it is not the big states that swing the election but several smaller ones.

Those states decide the election. All other states are assumed fixed in their respective outcomes, red or blue.

What we have is one strike against the electoral college system.

Significant numbers seemingly do not count, to the dismay of New York and California.

However, every issue has two sides. In this case, we have the problem of "the flyover states," the country's middle. Some of them enjoy the privilege of not only being a flyover state but also a swing state. So they are essential to typically both presidential campaigns.

Kudos to the electoral college system!

A few **maybe** options

Maybe we ought to consider having a unified voting process for the entire United States in federal elections defined in a bipartisan manner. Let the states do their thing in state and local elections.

Maybe voting for federal offices should be governed by federal law.

Maybe mail-in voting should only be part of the process under just extremely exceptional conditions. Allow it only if the condition of WHO and HOW is known and controlled.

Maybe making the voting process as easy as possible should not be one of the primary considerations.

Maybe worrying about foreign interference in our elections is not our top election problem.

Maybe cleaning up all our domestic voting issues is the most critical task at hand.

Maybe we can define one consistent voting process for all states.

Maybe the in-person voting process is the only reliable and trustworthy process for all elections.

Maybe a statement of a politician four weeks before a Senate runoff in Georgia, "I have 800,000 votes," should instill concern about legitimacy in any voter.

Notes:

_____

_____

_____

_____

_____

Workable Solutions to All Social Paradoxes

Numerous social concerns dominate our daily lives. Situations like caring for others less fortunate are one of them. People with a different philosophical perspective bombard us continuously. One side claims that the government is the solution while, at the same time, demonizing the other side as being insensitive, uncaring, greedy, and the like. The other side is arguing that individual responsibility is the solution to such problems. Yet despite significant efforts and expenditures, the issues stay or, even worse, grow even more critical with no end in sight. We spend a lot of effort but seem to fail in achieving a lasting desirable solution.

Chemical engineers have a term for such processes, steady state! We run at a steady state when the critical governing-control parameter of a process stays constant within given tolerances over time, even though various noncritical factors or variables introduce small insignificant changes.

Maybe our social engineer could learn a thing or two by finding the critical factors in our social systems!

Paradoxically, a paradox explains the failure of our efforts.

The wealth redistribution paradox. The more we redistribute money from more fortunate to less fortunate people, the longer it takes to decrease the less fortunate population or, even worse, increase its population.

We could also name it **the "maintain your poverty" paradox.**

The greater the number of poor people, the higher the demand for government intervention, which in turn keeps the poor "poor"!

Why do we face such a paradox?

Let me suggest a couple of simple questions.

Do you think our society is socially just?

Do you think we, as a society, can create a more socially just society?

Which aspects of our community would you change by what means to bring about the desired change?

The answers to these simple questions would ask for a broad range of responses. Your political philosophy and your standing within our society are the critical determinants for your replies. The answers would cover a wide range of solutions, each of which claimed to be an all-inclusive solution! Yet based on our intuition, we all know that there is typically only one optimum solution for any given problem. Our life experience teaches us this fact. How do we go ahead to put our thoughts on the right footing to bring about social justice or social equality or merely a more socially just society?

Let us look at anecdotal evidence!

In the sixties, the "War on Poverty" was put onto the books in the form of government programs that help the poor and less fortunate citizens through a wide range of subsidy payments.

Over roughly fifty years, the US government spent the gigantic sum of $20 trillion (about $62,000 per person in the US), yet the poverty rate remained virtually constant during all those years.

Nothing fundamentally changed according to the government stats that reflect this fact. One must presume the idea of such subsidies is

"to lift people out of poverty,"

by supplying a helping hand. On the other hand,

if we define success as the act of taking from the more fortunate and giving to the less fortunate,

then success is at hand. However, there is a problem with terminology: We happen to use the term

"War on Poverty"
and not
"War on Affluence"

to define success.

The United States of America is by far the wealthiest nation on earth by having an economy that is 25 percent of the world's gross national product. Its tax receipts aggregate in trillions while all other economies deal with mere billions. The absolute amount of tax revenues for the most current year are the highest ever. Those revenues are insufficient to cover all its expenditures by about 30 percent despite these favorable conditions!

Why would this be the case?

The wealthiest nation on the planet spends more than it takes in. Does that make sense? A brief look at the expenditure components shows that social entitlements such as Medicare, Medicaid, and Social Security and national security concerns are the primary sources of the permanent deficit. On top of those observations, the United States is socially deficient in our European allies' eyes.

> *Here we are, the wealthiest nation globally, socially deficient in others' eyes, and financially crushed by our deficient social entitlement obligations.*

None of the preceding is news to anybody. However, if we start with a different premise, we might be able to solve the problem. Maybe we must step back from thinking about the current state reflected by questions like how many poor people we have and how we can give them money to ease their pain. Alternatively, looking at the other side of the perceived problem, how few superrich people control what amount of money? Actions resulting from these questions have historically not contributed to a solution toward a socially just society.

However, if we ask a different question, we might solve an extraordinarily complex set of problems.

> *To do this, we must avoid thinking about our social issues and their piecemeal solutions and move toward thinking about defining our desired society's ideal or model state.*

It starts from the ground up and not from the top down. And it involves the definition of an ideal lowest member of our society.

What attributes does such a member need in the perfect case?

Given that we can do this in a specific form, we have a basis for our model society and define measures to transform our society and move toward the ideal or model case. That said, let us do it and express those ideal attributes for the lowest productive member of our perfect society.

What are the required attributes?

Self-sufficient: Meaning no outside support is needed.

Educated: Has acquired knowledge and skills that support self-sufficiency.

Productive: Applies knowledge and skills for his/her contributions to society.

Social: Interacts with others and aids as needed.

If we aggregate all our members of our ideal society, we have a culture that tries to preserve its perfect state. To do this, we must define measures and policies that move its members toward the ideal state as part of its self-preserving principles.

Furthermore, we must recognize that the respective aggregate in each principal part—self-sufficiency, education, productivity, and social interaction—have a variance of some kind.

This recognition implies that there is no such thing as an egalitarian society.

Each member of such a community makes various contributions resulting in varying but fair rewards.

Having derived such a simple model for our ideal society, we are ready to consider some of the consequences that move us away from our first paradoxes.

The wealth redistribution paradox or the "maintain your poverty" paradox.

It reflects the focus on inequality in wealth or earnings or status within our current society and top-down remedies. Not only have these measures proven to be ineffective, but they have shown to be contributors toward the expansion of the said problem.

Let us just look at some of the consequences. We know that we want every member of our society to be a contributing member! To achieve this aim, we must set up policies that supply a high success rate toward our goal. Let us look at some of the critical components of education, productivity, and social interaction and define some policy consequences.

Education:

- *Education is a mandatory part of our society and, as such, cannot be discretionary for any individual member of said society, and our policies need to reflect this condition.*
- *We can expect that increasing education expenditures and resulting increases in our society's productive members will reduce our corrective institutions' expenses.*
- *We need to be willing to supply similar education levels to all strata to break poverty cycles.*
- *If the rich are eager to educate their offspring away from home, the same should occur for the less-fortunate members of our society.*
- *We need to educate based on the aptitude of a given pupil. Our goal is to educate toward creating productive members of our society, manual skills for some, and intellectual skills for others in a cost-effective process.*

Productivity:

- *We aim to create a nearly 100 percent productive society. It implies that measures must take place that addresses the less-fortunate members of our community. Each member must contribute, regardless of how little, to instill a sense of self-satisfaction.*

Social interaction:

- *Policies must support the individual as opposed to the individual supporting the systems.*
- *We must perfect the social interaction of each member of our society and supply incentives to help others.*
- *We must create a society that uses its members to advance all areas of science, art, and the economy and supply a better place for generations to come.*

*****Our aim should be to make the wealth redistribution paradox obsolete.*****

What Next?

Okay, paradoxes are plentiful and reasonably practical ways to look at our problems from a different perspective. I hope you, the reader, feel that way too! They seem to open our eyes and help us look, even very familiar things, from a completely different perspective.

I know all of that is dry and tedious stuff, and if you reached this point, you deserve a reward, the Pavlovian kind!

That said, let's go on to the gems embedded in this book. What are those, you might ask?

*****Oxymorons, of course!*****

Please relax and enjoy them for what they are, in most cases, an unintentional contribution to humor by the originators.

Notes:

_____

_____

_____

_____

_____

A Few Oxymorons for
Your Enjoyment

We went ahead from symptoms to paradoxes and now have reached oxymorons.

Let us call it a logical progression.

While symptoms show a patchwork of unrelated problems and issues, in contrast, paradoxes may or may not lead to solutions.

On the other hand, oxymorons do not lead to any answers; quite the opposite. They are the antithesis of a solution. But they are the gems, rare and sometimes funny, and, if found, should be preserved for generations to enjoy.

So we know symptoms are plentiful, as are paradoxes, but oxymorons are few and are the gems that add spice to the political speech.

And in the worst case…

Oxymorons used by morons result in practical political speech and are pretty helpful for a clever tweet.

Let us go up the learning curve and look at relevant oxymorons.

Notes:

_____

_____

_____

_____

_____

Mark Zuckerberg Oxymoron

Mark Zuckerberg, the cofounder and prominent billionaire of Facebook fortune, prides himself on his X billion users' fair treatment on his platform. While this behavior might be correct for some of his constituents, it is not valid for all.

Zuckerberg contends that Facebook is not an arbiter of truth.
Kudos to Mark.

Yet in the case of some *hydroxychloroquine* reporting he disagreed with, he restated his position and, knowingly or unknowingly, created a delightful gem, a precious oxymoron.

Facebook is not the arbitrator of truth but does drop misleading facts from its platform!

Who says Mark Zuckerberg is not funny!

Notes:

_____

_____

_____

_____

_____

Paid Rioter Oxymoron

Paid rioters seem to pop up every time a grave issue surfaces. A race issue is typically at the origin. The murderers of Reverend Martin Luther King, Rodney King, and George Floyd were the cause of those explosions. People launching protests are peaceful for a while and then get bored; and riots, destruction, and lootings appear!

And here they are, the paid protestors armed with Molotov cocktails, baseball bats, torches, gasoline cans, high-powered lasers, bricks, and anything helpful in injuring, permanently debilitating, and killing people. Their sole intent is destroying private or public property and inflicting as much pain or permanent damage as possible.

Just out of curiosity, there is a question of interest.

What is the hourly pay rate of paid protesters? More significantly, who keeps the time sheet?

We may never know, and even more importantly, the source of funds used for payment.

We know for sure that those paid protestors, or better-defined rioters, are organized, live in the dark, and hide behind masks and shields. Anonymity is what they look for and get if the justified protest rules allow all those destructive tools.

If asked why they do what they do, we might get an answer like this.

> **Our protests—riots, looting, maiming, and destruction notwithstanding—are for a better future!**

Only morons and anonymous funders can produce such a gem!

Notes:

_____

_____

_____

_____

_____

Racist Oxymoron

Race relations are an untouchable subject, particularly for the majority of White population. Most of them belong proudly to the silent majority, characterized by never voicing an opinion publicly.

> **Those people elected the first Black President, hoping and praying the race issue would go away.**

Dreaming that the first Black President can clean up this ever-present scourge of racism in US history.

The short answer is no, he could not.

It got worse! How?

Now any White citizen expressing anything contrary to the current Democratic Party line is, by definition, a racist. It is called White privilege.

Racist promoters like Al Sharpton make sure that this topic never goes away. And it will not if he has anything to say about it!

But there is hope!

Mind you, only a tiny glimmer, as we find the precious gem, the oxymoron.

The more we call the majority racists, the better our future race relations.

Good luck, Al!

Notes:

_____

_____

_____

_____

_____

Amazon/AOC Oxymoron

Alexandria Ocasio-Cortez, aka AOC. Her rise to power is nothing short of amazing. A college-educated bartender defeats a trillion-term House representative in the NY Democratic Party primary. Her first move in Washington was to stage a sit-in at the Speaker's office. Then she gathered another million Twitter followers, signaling to everyone, "I am here, and I am serious!"

AOC has another little trait. She has an eye for fashion, expensive and very stylish fashion—style not to be found in any discount store. As a prudent socialist, she goes to secondhand high-fashion stores to buy her type of clothing.

By doing so, she subsidizes the rich and famous;
she despises on ideological grounds.

She is not aware that her future dream world, a socialist paradise of equality, does not create and produce high fashion; only those greedy capitalist pigs do!

Success in her mission to install socialism will create a dilemma for her. Best described by a seventies TV ad showing several *Tamara Press*-looking women in drab dresses on the fashion runway using the tagline "*Is sick Russian beauty queen!*"

All that success did not come about by being a thinker and distributor of profound thought. For example, look at her Amazon New York headquarters position. While many cities throughout the US were trying to lure Amazon into their midst, AOC was not for it. The potential 50,000 jobs with a projected average salary of $100,000 did not impress her, far from it.

She was against NY, giving Amazon a big tax break. And here it is, our precious gem.

We can spend the Amazon tax reductions on
much more meaningful projects.

While her intent might very well have been sincere, her sense of reality is not. Amazon cut bait and opted to avoid any future conflict with AOC.

No New York headquarters,
No 50,000 new jobs, and
No tax revenue to spend on more appropriate projects.

What should we conclude from all of that? It is hard to say. Did she rise to power too fast, or what is more accurate?

Is a moron just a moron?

Notes:

_____

_____

_____

_____

Capitalism/AOC Oxymoron

If there is one thing about AOC, she is not bashful or shy, venturing into the domain of established thought. She is an open supporter of Karl Marx's ideas, even a charter member of his fan club. She does not seem to be bothered, by the fact, that none of Karl's ideas ever worked.

So, what, just a nitpicking detail?

Being a believing supporter of socialism, it is her calling to attack its archenemy, capitalism.

Not by way of slander and insults but with her profound thought and logic.

So she started to question the fundamental assumptions made by capitalists.

Here it is, her revolutionizing thought that will change our capitalist economic structure forever.

The fundamental notion of capitalism is scarce resources. This notion is not valid any longer as we have virtually unlimited resources.

Now why have we not thought of such profound insight before?

Well, in her former business setting, after two martinis and a few shots for scotch, this idea makes sense.

Otherwise, we must file it away together with *"perpetual motion." C'est la vie*, another innovative idea that went bad.

On the bright side, we genuinely have another gem, a precious oxymoron, boldly expressed by a moron.

Where Do We Go from Here?

It seems you, the reader, have been able to relax and enjoy the precious few gems and are now ready and able to become sober again.

Let's recap; we look at problems in the form of symptoms, paradoxes, and oxymorons from various perspectives!

That was helpful but insufficient.

What is missing?

A rigorous definition of the problems we intend to solve together!

Notes:

_____

_____

_____

_____

_____

WHAT ARE THE CURRENT FUNDAMENTAL PROBLEMS?

Private and Public Sector Interaction!

Thus far, our journey together through a patchwork or quilt of indicators, symptoms, paradoxes, and oxymorons has not yielded any unanimously agreed optimum solution. Now why would that be?

Well, it would be a brilliant idea to define the root cause of the problem.

Now how do we do that?

What do we know, and how can we apply our knowledge?

Typically, problem definition can be *bottom-up* or *top-down*. Our journey thus far was mired in the swamp, and our result is, accordingly, covered with mud. We met lots of issues and problems but no viable optimum solutions for any of them.

Let me repeat a suitable phrase.

> **When you're up to your ass in an alligator, it is hard to recall that the original goal was to drain the swamp!**

Enough said.

Let us go to the top.

How far, you might ask?

We need to go to the very top.

Because we would like to look down, for a change, and not get covered in mud to cloud our vision, our judgment as well.

From the top, we see an economic system composed of two sectors, public and private.

> *And we notice right away that the public sector has too much control over the private sector.*

And we also see, as noted before,

> *the public sector spends money, and the private sector generates wealth.*

That observation will help us to get the ball rolling.

There is no point in dealing with the public sector; politicians, bureaucrats, and lobbyists already do a bang-up job and help spend all that money they do not have, even though there are immense problems within that sector.

Problems like

- *huge annual budget deficits,*
- *huge trade deficits,*
- *unsustainable social payments,*
- *government wasteful spending,*
- *exponentially growing bureaucracy, and*
- *no effort to address any of it!*

> *Maybe we can help ANTIFA switch its focus of destruction from the private sector to the public sector.*

That would be accommodating!
Our focus must be on the private sector.
Why focus on it?

> *It generates the nation's wealth in ever-increasing value!*
>
> *And it is the most potent wealth-generation engine ever conceived by humankind!*

It allows upward mobility for anyone from meager beginnings or poverty to the wealthiest person in the universe! So what is the problem?

For example, Jeff Bezos, the richest man in the world, created Amazon and by doing so, is immensely rewarded for it. Everyone knows those facts, but the following circumstances are more exciting and revealing.

During his initial testimony at a Congressional Committee, he said his mother was a seventeen-year-old high school student who met considerable school resistance. As a young unwed mother, she was not allowed to attend graduation.

Only in America can a boy growing up, under those circumstances, become the wealthiest man in the world.

So back to our task at hand, who or what controls the private sector?

Politicians, bureaucrats, lobbyists, and individual entities are called corporations.

It is a trick question.

The correct answer is nobody!

Politicians assert considerable influence over the private sector.

Most of their contributions are negative. Seldom or virtually never do they use lubricants; they resort to bricks and sand to make their contributions in the form of regulations and higher taxes.

Bureaucrats are likewise in the obstacle business as they enforce regulations or tighten interest rates or change money flows.

But at times, they can be helpful by lowering interest rates or relaxing money flows.

The lobbyists are different altogether.

> *They are in the business of monetizing their experience gained in the various government structures by actively influencing their former coworkers in legal but not so ethical ways.*

Concisely, lobbying is the Western form of legalized corruption.

Individual corporations or business sectors derive value by influencing the creation of new laws and regulations.

Corporations take all the earlier structures and find ways and means to maximize the outcome of their objectives. The result may or may not be suitable for the country as the various problem areas during the COVID-19 crisis have sufficiently demonstrated.

> *Optimum supply chains of a critical product or service from only one source may not be in the country's best interest if the trading partner is both your only supplier and your greatest adversary.*

Suppose a vast number of corporate decisions have some of these components. In that case, the unlimited freedom to act and decide, the free enterprise system's greatest strength, also becomes its "Achilles heel."

There is an overall optimum for the private sector, and nobody oversees it! See COVID-19 example.

Corporations do what corporations do best: perfect the outcome within their domain!

Let us discuss some low-hanging-fruit problems!

Notes:

_____

_____

_____

_____

_____

How Do We Get an Educated Workforce?

The current approach is one of "laissez-faire." Individuals select a trade, study a subject or calling, and then hope that the demand of businesses or institutions for the acquired expertise is given and rewarded.

Both sides are rolling the dice and hope that everything will work out for the best.

On top of it, selecting a vocation or calling might sound enticing for an eighteen-year-old high school graduate but may or may not have any prospects for adequate future income. Worse yet, some of the chosen exotic study subjects, financed with considerable back-breaking debt and no successful financial future insight, put the hopeful contributor into a state of despair from the start.

"Another life ruined by our greedy capitalistic society," proclaimed by the socialists, might find resonance within the desperate and young.

We know that this kind of desperation is entirely avoidable and should not happen at all. But it does.

The chosen "laissez-faire" approach does not supply sufficient guidance, particularly for future demand for various white- and blue-collar skills and knowledge.

Yes, there is a problem with a young prospect's poor choices, but there is an even bigger problem of not having access to demand projected over a ten-to-twenty-year horizon.

Given we expect skills shortages as a way of life, we are okay!

If not, we ought to do something about it.

Here, we can learn a thing or two from the public sector. Let us look at our military institutions. All of them develop their leadership cadre via top-notch academies. All students are on scholarships and must commit to serving for a minimum time horizon after graduation. None is in debt after graduation! And there is no shortage of applicants; the institutions get the pick of the litter. The systems work to perfection, and the US military is second to none across the globe.

The private sector has nothing like it from a global perspective.

Even though there are distinct requirements for skilled human resources for any given year, no such comprehensive plan exists.

Notes:

_____

_____

_____

_____

_____

How Do We Acquire, Keep, and Support Our Workforce?

There is the apparent answer: pay and reward the employee competitively.

Such a response can be sufficient and, at the same time, become the problem of our societal structure.

Given that we negotiate everything, we must expect that some fare better than others, and such outcomes can be significant problems. Intentional or unintentional, it does not matter.

The notion of different health-care types offered to the various levels within an organization would lead to internal and external protests—none of them beneficial for the corporate entity. So we must be careful where we compete and how we differentiate.

Our current structure allows competition in all aspects of attracting and rewarding employees.

So far, so good!

Individuals have different expectations and desires; thus, other outcomes are the result. However, there are some essential issues: health care and minimum or working wage.

Those are the red-meat leftists' issues!

The absence of both creates social turmoil, arguably so. Modern wealthy societies should not have any of those issues.

> *First, it is in society's own best interest to have and keep a healthy population.*
> *Second, all jobs, at a minimum, should pay a self-supporting wage.*

It could not get any easier.

Yet the failure of having no minimum standards create constant underlying dissatisfaction. The public sector—in particular, some left-leaning politicians, such as our millionaire socialist, Senator Bernie Sanders—have made it their calling to poke the eyes of the private sector regularly. The considerable following, from college-educated young people, should be a dire warning.

But it is not!

So the private sector must fend off the efforts of the left on a turnstile basis. Over and over and over again, with no permanent solution in sight.

> *Solving those two issues will make obsolete Senator Bernie Sanders and his conspirators,*

> *the Marxist college professors, poison our igno-*
> *rant and naive students.*

The outcome is a win for everybody, the private sector, and its workers.

Thus, not all competition is brilliant, and external intervention from the public sector is not helpful.

> *The private sector should not relinquish con-*
> *trol to the public sector for ill-chosen bonehead*
> *decisions.*

Notes:

_____

_____

_____

_____

How Do We Distribute the Profits?

Recall Churchill's brilliant quote, again for good measure.

> *"The inherent vice of capitalism is the unequal*
> *sharing of blessings; the inherent virtue of*
> *socialism is the equal sharing of miseries."*

Let us deal with the capitalist *"the unequal sharing of blessings"* and assess our current situation—short answer.
Not too good!

> *We tolerate million-dollar rewards for exec-*
> *utives, while at the same time, a corporation*
> *does not pay a self-supporting wage to some of*
> *its employees.*

Accepting such a social structure cannot be a good thing for the private sector eventually.

Why, you might ask?

> **The failure to pay a self-supporting wage to a single individual will transfer the problem solution to the public sector to compensate via a subsidy in one form or another.**

However, this is only one part of the problem.

Accepting such practices will supply convenient cannon fodder to Senator Bernie Sanders-like socialists.

He is not alone; let us not forget AOC and her comrades.

Beware!

The comrades are eager to destroy the most productive wealth-generation system ever created, initially with creativity-stifling regulations and laws and later, with their trump card, Marxist socialism.

Can it happen?

Hell, yes, it can!

Our higher-learning institutions, claiming to be a place for discussion of all ideas, are a breeding ground of lousy ideas and filtered thoughts.

> **If it is not liberal, we do not want to discuss it!**

Just look at the personal. For every conservative professor, there are at least ten Marxist professors if there is such a thing. And they aim to poison the minds of naive and workable students.

Are they successful?

Hell, yes, just look at the swelling ranks of ANTIFA.

And the naive and proud successful alumni are still funding that cesspool of rubbish thought. They always dream of their time at this former magic place called University XYZ and their football team's successes. No conditions, just millions and millions of dollars handed over to fund, among other things, the Marxists' salaries.

Alumni, wake up and do what made you successful.

*** Think, formulate, and demand!***

And finally, only donate if you understand the use of your generous funds!

Another thought, speaking of Marxist profs!

Have you ever gotten any proposal of a solution from the existing Marxist dogma superior to our free enterprise system?

Answer: Nada, zero, nothing!

They only know how to reiterate Marx and Lenin and those who need that education in failure.

Parton me: We ought to be aware of one success. The socialist Hugo Chaves's daughter is a documented billionaire with a capital B. (Not bad for sharing miseries!)

We Made Progress, but What Next?

There is one solitary thing we can take to heart. Just knowing all the problems does not lead us to the desired solutions.

What will guide you toward a solution?

By defining an all-encompassing goal for the private sector!

So let us go on and do just that!

Notes:

_____

_____

_____

_____

_____

What Is the Solution?

The patchwork of observations affords us some conclusions that might lead to root-cause problem solutions.

For instance, looking at the public sector, we notice its structure, organization, rules, laws, faults, advantages, and direct influence and control of the private sector.

Doing the same for the private sector, we find nothing even close to the public sector structure.

So one thing is clear: Politicians and bureaucrats, to a significant degree, can influence and control the private sector.

It is in the form of

- *regulations,*
- *tax rates and taxable events,*
- *import or export restrictions,*
- *social-service obligations, and*
- *other miscellaneous items.*

The private sector is agile and adapts its operations accordingly, not as a single organized unit but as an industrial sector or single corporation.

In either case, the resulting required changes are not yielding the best solutions. They are what they are, suboptimal solutions to obstacles presented by the public sector. Additionally, those presented obstacles are politically tainted by those who occupy the political power for the moment. They may or may not change in six-year or four-year or, the worst case, two-year intervals.

Politicians can create obstacles for the private sector as part of their appeal for the next political campaign. Recall those slogans.

> *Increase the taxes for corporations!*
> *Let us ensure that the purple canary habitat is not disturbed before we grant building the Oklahoma pipeline!*
> *Tax the millionaires and billionaires!*
> *And the beat goes on!*

And they do and quite often. And the outcome is always the same: a suboptimal solution for the private sector. One party says "hue" with an unusual move to the left, and the other party says "hot"; and to the right we go.

Begging the question, "There ought to be a better way?"

And there is!

Let us start with the goal of the private sector. May I suggest a simple one:

Control the destiny of all aspects of the private sector operation!

Now would not that be nice!

And what are its implications?

Overwhelming and far-reaching, for sure!

In Principle, Two Organizational Issues Beg for a Solution

First, the private sector must get organized and set up an umbrella organization. Control sug-

gests organization, which implies an umbrella organization that includes all its entities.

The specific organizational solution is not too important if it is fully democratic and not overly bureaucratic.

Slim, agile, efficient, and effective would be nice-to-have characteristics.

The failure of not having such an organization allows politicians to use the private sector as their piggy bank, their perpetual bad boy and troublemaker and their whipping boy.

No more!

Second, the private sector must set up a third political party. Let us call it the Independent Party, a political party standing for the private sector's interests, in concert with the Independent voter.

With sufficient representation in both House and Senate, the private sector can become the swing vote on any issue and align with either party on any topic.

Remember, it is all about "control of destiny."

One word of caution! It makes sense that politicians of any stripe may not be in favor of relinquishing any of their presently exercised control!

Robust and viable third-party presence can end the tried-and-true Washington method of bickering and stalemate and replace it with progress on any issue to better the entire nation.

Isn't it exciting!

Creating two simple organizations can solve a boatload of chronic problems.

But what is even more appealing is, those two changes have secondary and tertiary consequences.
And that is where the real power of the transformation becomes known.

It is easy to talk about actual direct results, consequences such as the following:

- *The private sector has a direct dialogue, at eye level, with established political power sources: House, Senate, and Executive.*
- *It has direct control over international business policies.*
- *It has the power to support its workforce from the cradle to the grave.*
- *It has the power to set up fair and just wealth and income distribution policies, just for starters.*

Before diving into the secondary and tertiary consequences, we need to revisit some of the most fundamental problems the country faces today and ask how an organized private sector can contribute or solve some of those problems.

As a refresher, what are some of the significant and insurmountable challenges?

1. *The federal government faces a perpetual budget deficit that neither party is either willing or able to address.*
2. *The national debt is climbing with no end in sight.*
3. *The country faces a perpetual trade deficit with no solution on the horizon.*
4. *The bureaucracy of the federal government always grows but never shrinks.*
5. *The country has yet to overcome its historical race problem. And none of the current approaches lead to any viable solution any time soon!*

We can agree those are big ones.

Thus far, neither administration, Democratic or Republican, is either willing or able or, most disturbing, even interested in solving any of those problems.

Let us talk about the nation's number one problem: the federal budget deficit. The private sector has no direct input on how the federal government spends its money.

Sadly enough, it only supplies the funds for it, and not enough, so it seems.

In general, politicians want to spend more of what they do not have, so they borrow. And the latest breed of progressives, who ought to be more appropriately named regressive, want to spend even more to save the planet by financially destroying the country and tripling the national debt.

Now how can the private sector help in the solution to the federal budget problem? There are two routes, directly and indirectly. The direct way is only supplying more money, but that has not helped one iota.

Giving more money to politicians creates only more demand for more spending!

We might as well burn it.

Here is where the indirect route is quite helpful. A practical Independent Party in both House and Senate would be a good start.

A balanced budget act would eventually pass with the votes of all financially prudent Democrats, Republicans, and Independents in both Houses.

Mind you, the dogmatic leadership postures within both established parties are a relic of a contentious past, where the party was more important than the country.

It is time to switch from dogmatic to pragmatic for all our politicians.

So the private sector can be a helpful driver for restoring financial sanity at the federal level.

All other ideas have thus far failed!

> **The third problem, the perpetual trade deficit, is a prototype private sector problem. And the private sector must address it with multidimensional solutions.**

For instance, which goods and services are exported and imported?

Which goods and services are strategic and require a certain percentage of domestic production?

Which goods and services require specific proprietary technology for export expansion?

You get the point.

Only a detailed assessment will supply the answers.

Next, let us address problem number four, the perpetual growing federal bureaucracy.

> **Solving problem number one, the persistent budget deficit by default, will deal with that issue. And our helpful third party, the Independence Party, will help to drain the swamp.**

The last problem on our list, the historic race problem, is the most difficult one to solve. Emotions go high from time to time when race-related killings occur.

> **The progression of protest, riot, looting, and burning has not brought about any solutions but made the typical race promoters rich and powerful.**

And, not too surprising, the cycle repeats itself in predictable time intervals.

Conclusion: We are high on emotions but empty on solutions.

And if we honestly and unemotionally look at the problem, we find an issue of low or no education, deplorable living conditions, neighborhoods filled with crime, and no prospects for any change for the near future.

Now what could go wrong under those circumstances!

Public sector-run programs spending $20 trillion over fifty years (about $62,000 per person in the US) in a war on poverty changed little as the poverty rate decreased by 1 percent.

All government programs seemed to have an unintended or intended destructive element, such as throwing the male out of the household, thereby creating 70 percent fatherless households.

Also, compassionate welfare payments given to poor souls will do nothing but damage the unfortunate recipients over many generations.

Compassion is a good thing but, applied by the government bureaucrats, can be an evil thing.

It seems none of the well-intended programs did address the root cause of problems: education, living conditions, crime, and no future.

So we protest, riot, loot, and burn to bring about change! Only to repeat the vicious cycle in a few years again and again.

Not too surprising, there are satisfied people. The ones who profit repeatedly. Those who consistently seek the limelight during and after the riots! Acting as change agents but never carrying out anything as any positive change destroys the profitable business model.

Now what can the private sector do differently from the government sector?

Plenty!

Break the cycle of poverty with a plan to convert welfare recipients into taxpayers.

For starters, teach skills needed to produce services and products. Locate manufacturing and services facilities close to the labor force. Build and subsidize affordable and decent housing nearby and end the cycle of crime.

Pay a self-supporting wage and change the protestor to a proud American taxpayer.

So an organized private sector can do a lot to solve historic public sector problems.

Surprise, surprise! And most noteworthy, without the help of progressive (regressive) transfer payment supporters.

How to Implement Structural Changes for the Private Sector

We identified the what and how and now face the implementation problem. And a big one it is.

Naturally, the bigger the problem, the bigger the change agent.

That said, why not go for, by far, the most successful American entrepreneurs in recent history?

Notes:

_____

_____

_____

_____

_____

Change Agents

Knowing what to change is only one side of the coin. Implementing the two suggested structural changes is another problem altogether.

It is akin to asking the Titanic *captain to change course while the iceberg is visible nearby!*

The two suggested organizational solutions stand for an immense challenge for the country. The problems are highly like the ones the European countries faced creating the EU. Their concern was much more complicated as twenty-seven independent countries tried to find a unifying solution of one joint overlying government structure.

And they did—an overly complicated bureaucratic maze.

So using the EU as a template is out. Yet they got one thing right.

> **The European countries did unite and did create the EU and have broken the historical paradigm of fighting each other in little and big wars or scrimmages.**

So they learned!

The EU lesson is a simple one. Find a few compassioned visionaries who have the experience, vision, and leadership to unite the private sector into one single, more powerful unit. The US has always had the great fortune of having visionaries who changed the world. Henry Ford, Thomas Edison, and Steve Jobs are some that come to mind as clear examples. Aside from being in various fields, they have another thing in common. They are all deceased. So we need to look at living and still active persons to find some current examples.

Are there any?
Yes, there are!

Bill Gates

Let us look at **Bill Gates**, the cofounder of Microsoft. He had the vision to quit Harvard and go back to the West Coast and be part of the microprocessor revolution. And a good revolution it was! Gates was the first one of the revolutionaries who saw the business aspect. His software solutions allowed his worldwide users to become more productive.

> *His vision connected the exploding semiconductor hardware innovations via his software solutions with the user.*

Some people estimated a 1–2 percent annual gain in productivity over a twenty-year horizon just for the US alone.

Big stuff!

Gates became the richest man in the world and, as a sideline, created about 12,000 Microsoft employee millionaires. Microsoft currently has approximately 117,000 employees worldwide, which is the most significant social deed of them all: *"give someone a job."*

Gates is now busy disposing of his vast fortune for charitable causes, most notably, third-world vaccinations.

> *So he still has vision, a boatload of valuable contacts, financial resources, and knows how to get difficult jobs done.*
> *Let us say a prototype change agent!*

Notes:

_____

_____

_____

_____

_____

Jeff Bezos

. . . .

Another one of the current sets of compassionate visionaries is **Jeff Bezos**, founder of Amazon. Reading and hearing about him in our "mainstream press," I encountered the nickname "Dr. Evil" while having no idea who he was as an individual. The eye-opener came at his first public testimony at one of House Judiciary subcommittees.

In his opening comments, Bezos talked about his mother, who had him while being at high school at the ripe old age of seventeen. He also mentioned that her pregnancy prohibited her from being allowed to the graduation ceremony. He went on to say that he, baby Jeff, was taken by her to night class to complete her high school education.

Remarkable, the now richest man in the world was growing up under those circumstances! A son was honoring his mother in front of the entire nation.

Remarkable!

What he did not say was what "Planned Parenthood" does to help a pregnant seventeen-year-old high school student. Given that prospect, what are the odds of a seventeen-year-old carrying a baby to terms? Not exceedingly high!

Remarkable!

In less than thirty years, Jeff Bezos created the most significant retailer globally in market capitalization. Amazon is one of a handful of trillion-dollar companies.

Remarkable!

While he started as an online bookseller, his vision morphed into an online company that sells virtually anything worldwide! He does it with an unprecedented customer focus. That is why Amazon is second to none!

Remarkable!

What is Jeff Bezos's social contribution? Jeff Bezos created about 840,000 jobs. Eight hundred forty thousand people taken of potentially government dependency and put into a position of self-sufficiency!

Remarkable!

In short, another prototype change agent!

Both are superstars in their chosen field, and both would be more than qualified to complete the mission. Are there others?

Are there other possible candidates who would qualify for leading this enormous task? There certainly are. So let's look at another highly successful individual to contrast our previously displayed suggested leaders. His name is George Soros, and he is currently busy spending some of his billions to change the world.

Notes:

_____

_____

_____

_____

_____

George Soros

Soros's journey through his ninety years is impressive and astonishing. His survival skills and instincts are second to none. Yet here is not the time and place to go through his tough formative years.

A few highlights will suffice! Most astonishingly, having the instinct to change the family name to slip through the NAZI dragnet and, on top of it, staying close to the NAZIS is even more daring. And, as this was not enough, after, encountering and escaping the Bolsheviks is another miracle. To top it off, having the drive and intellect to pursue and complete his education in the West after leaving communist Hungary behind is nothing short of spectacular.

So Soros is a tough cookie and a born survivor!

And what is even more astonishing is, this escapee from totalitarian communism transforms into the quintessential capitalist. Yes, George Soros is not settling for being second; he becomes number one!

George Soros becomes the capitalist of capitalists.

The one who recognizes and seizes every opportunity for instant speculative gains. His ultimate achievement, as phrased by the press? He became *the man who broke the bank of England!*

He gained $1 billion (about the cost of an inexpensive major league baseball team), while many little people lost their life savings. Nothing new in capitalistic societies; George Soros simply was more astute, insightful, and faster than everybody else. He became one of the most successful speculators in modern financial history.

He became what every genuine capitalist wants to be: a multibillionaire.

Soros was different from the other two change agents; his gains were other people's losses. He did not create thousands of new jobs, nor did he make a new industry due to his life's work.

Only money changed hands, primarily into his hands!

Having all those billions, Soros entered the arena of philanthropy. He formed the Open Society Foundations and funded it with his surplus billions.

And that is where the rubber hits the road.

We can characterize Soros's engagement as a metamorphosis from kingpin capitalist to compassionate socialist, social thinker, or unrestricted free-society proponent, a globalist.

So he is a globalist who supports any progressive cause there is!

Consequently, he supports ANTIFA, an organization aimed at changing society through destruction. Yet that organization, visible through their black uniforms, is eerily like the brown uniforms worn by NAZIS, destroying Jews shops and houses during the "Kristallnacht" in NAZI Germany.

Is it so difficult to see the correlation?

Fortunately, ANTIFA does not have the broad-based support the NAZIS enjoyed. Thank god! Otherwise, they would do likewise and start the killing, which they do, fortunately, only in rare circumstances and small numbers. But they kill!

So he has not changed; he still is an opportunist, a soft-hearted champion of social causes, a destroyer of existing social structures, and by no means a builder.

He is still an opportunist who is leading from behind.

"Leading from behind"—now where did we hear that phrase? Ah, the Obama oxymoron!

The second destructive organization is "Black Lives Matter." They sound convincing and practical, but they do not live up to their billing.

George Soros funds them, hopefully with the intent to end the racial discrimination in America. Unfortunately, Black Lives Matter is not addressing the underlying root causes.

They are more into the destruction of the "White American society!"

Another good fit for George.

What is the root cause of the race problem?

- *Inferior education*
- *Deplorable living conditions*
- *Single-mother family structure*
- *High local crime rates*
- *No job prospects*
- *No future-earnings prospect*

Permanent solutions to those problems would solve a substantial part of the "race problem." How simple can it be?

The Black Lives Matter organization is worth another, more in-depth look. They principally originated in response to "White police killing Black citizens." Unfortunately, those killings receive disproportionate press coverage, leaving the impression of being a rampant problem, which it is not. The number of cases in one year may or may not exceed twenty plus for any given year. So we have a problem, but not a systematic, structural problem. Those facts do not bother the Black Lives Matter organization. Neither the fact that Blacks kill most Blacks. That problem is about a hundred times greater than the problem addressed by Black Lives Matter.

The Whites and Hispanics do likewise, so there is no surprise. What is surprising is that we ignore the massive problem and pursue the minor issues to no end.

So what is the reason?

An organization like Black Lives Matter could not collect a dime from people like George Soros on the broad issue.

Poor, desperate people killing each other does not report or print well in our current mainstream press configuration.

But White racist anti-Black police killing an innocent poor Black victim can drive the news cycle for months or years, particularly if protests, riots, and looting ensued.

It is hard to see which goal George Soros pursues; whatever the outcome, there will be no structural gain due to his contribution.

According to the Open Society Foundations website, they currently fund about 5,600 active projects, actions, causes, etc. worldwide. That is impressive, or is it?

Such a number suggests extraordinary compassion for a broad spectrum of fundamental problems; that is not the question.

But none of those vast causes seemed to create a permanent structural solution in any undertakings, at least they do not claim any such solutions.

Yet all of that should be no surprise as virtually all his many members of various committees are intellectuals of diverse kinds,

typically not used to building stuff but firmly entrenched in the arguing business.

So the difference between the mentioned change agents could not be any more significant. The first two created thousands of jobs and enhanced the lives of their respective employees and customers. A win-win for everyone.

Both Gates and Bezos created a new industry by offering innovative products or services to their customers.

The downside? Both companies, Microsoft and Amazon, are virtual monopolies in some businesses.

None of that applies to George Soros. All of George Soros's transactions were win-lose in their outcome.

Finally, they have only one thing in common: They are all billionaires!

All that said, let's look at the task at hand.

Which is, to create an inclusive umbrella organization for the private sector that can solve fundamental problems.

The organization formation cannot be the goal. Adding another layer of bureaucracy has never added any value anywhere—however, our purpose does.

Control the destiny of all aspects of the private sector operation!

Before exploring the essential options and issues, we must set the private sector boundary before going on a journey.

Let us consider the private sector as a closed system—meaning, it must have the ability to act on its own without any external interaction.

In plain English, it must not rely on any outside support, such as subsidies like pensions, health-care benefits, and welfare payments, to cite a few examples from the public sector, the government.

Let us explore the possible consequences of such a change. And to abuse a common phrase, "The sky is the limit!"

One word of caution: We cannot expect to predict all advantages and disadvantages resulting from that immense change.

Nobody can!

Except for AOC. She can envision a world without fossil fuel, airplanes, any pollution, and no adverse consequences as a result—the only downside is a great xx trillion-dollar price tag.

A small price to pay for Nirvana!

Is she a descendent of Nostradamus?

Anyone?

Now let us go to the fun part of our exercise. What consequences can we expect because of the organizational change?

Huge changes!

Notes:

_____

_____

_____

_____

_____

Finding Solutions for Existing Problems

Let us see what our socialist comrades say to discredit capitalism and explore if viable and sustainable solutions are possible.

Let us start with the underlying issues, the social ones, that unite all socialists, leftists, progressives, conservatives, and even some dictators. Maduro of Venezuela comes to mind.

Principally, nobody wants to see social injustice!

There are exceptions—those who steal foreign aid, like Arafat, or simply permanently borrow from the state, like Hugo Chavez.

It is only the difference between saying and doing. A trivial matter that the masses do not detect, so it appears.

> *What we know is that conservatives donate more to charities than liberals.*

Why?

> *Conservatives believe in individual responsibility and liberals in government solutions primarily through taxation.*

Each is doing what they think! Thus, there is no great surprise.

Now is the chance to demonstrate that the private sector can find better and define more permanent solutions.

So let us get to it!

Notes:

_____

_____

_____

_____

It Is a Disgrace for a Rich Country to Pay a Wage to Some Laborers Insufficient for Survival!

"Laborers on the bottom end of the spectrum cannot earn **a living wage**," like what Bernie Sanders, our favorite millionaire socialist, calls it.

Is he right? Or is he wrong?

He is suitable for some industries and wrong for others. That is the short answer! Comrade AOC would chime in by echoing Bernie's observations.

> *Their solution: Let the government define the "minimum-wage structure."*

Is that what the private sector needs?

Increased government interference and regulations and the accompanying government control by politicians!

Yes, we can see why Bernie and AOC like that solution.

More political power!

Bernie and AOC are only the visible leadership of that line of thought using Karl Marx's recipe for failure. They are trying to apply it to solve our current problems. And those two are not alone, and they have compatriots.

> *Their allies live in the ivory towers of our major universities, dispensing intellectual rubbish and poisoning the workable minds of their highly gullible students.*

Are these efforts successful? Increased participants in social issues rallies say yes!

Let us go back to our original problem.

What is wrong with a strict market solution?

> *Not paying hardworking laborers enough with a self-supporting wage is the fuse on a social and political powder keg.*

Recognizing this fact and not doing anything about it is akin to tempting the opposition to light it. Let there be no doubt; the opponents will do so at an opportune moment.

Why is it the #1 issue?

It fits the central Marxist narrative: exploitation of labor by capitalists. Now that is a mouthful: **wealthy capitalists exploiting weak labor for their financial gains.** That is why this must be a nonissue.

> *Any solution must err on the generous side.*

It is much better to pay too much than not enough! The gain is a much more stable and productive society.

Are there any alternative solutions?

Yes, there are! We simply must set a few guidelines.

Definition: The self-supporting wage will allow an individual to live under decent conditions without a government or any other SUBSIDY.

It will adhere to what society expects as a minimum standard of living.

The self-supporting wage will be different by region based on the regional cost of living.

The private sector will figure out, watch, and control the self-supporting wage—an enormous difference from our current public sector efforts.

Setting a self-supporting wage for the agriculture sector or any other low-skill labor sector will require a slight increase in consumer prices domestically, thereby adjusting import products.

A small price to pay for social stability!

Notes:

_____

_____

_____

_____

_____

China Syndrome

I am stealing a memorable line to make a point. Not that we are on the brink of a nuclear confrontation, far from it! China is our trading partner, and we, Western free enterprise, are doing our best to squeeze every dollar out of that relationship!

Or is it the other way around?

Pre-Nixon life in China was not a pretty picture.

China then was an economic nobody.

Only bicycles occupied the streets.

All people wore blue cotton outfits as the Chinese, presumably, did not have a sense of fashion.

All borders were locked tight, and no international trade took place.

Hunger and famine were part of daily living for the billion-plus peasants.

No advanced technology existed anywhere.

A lot has changed since Nixon's first visit to China.

China is the biggest exporter in the world.

Cities have exploded and are looking like Western metropolitan areas.

China adopted a central control "FREE" enterprise model.

China forces Western companies to "SHARE" their technology with their Chinese counterparts.

China has transformed itself from an agrarian economy to a high-technology economy!

Most importantly, China does not respect the intellectual property rights of others.

However, some things remained constant in Chinese life.

Communists are still in power.

Democracy is still a dream.

Human rights, nowhere to be seen! Who needs that Western concept!

Concentration camps for minorities instead!

To sum it up, I must steal another movie line: It is the good, the bad, and the ugly from a Western perspective.

And there is another critical observation we must make. China does not commit all its despicable and self-serving illegal business transactions on its own.

They simply could not do it.

They need a partner in crime, and it is the greed and short-term profit motive of the independently working private sector, the multinational corporations.

Those short-term motives indirectly support many goals of the Chinese Communist Party. Let us look at those.

The biggest sin the world's private sectors committed, as a team, is financing the Communist China expansion!

Its military growth, not directly but indirectly through the annual trade deficit.

The US contribution to the deficit is a paltry $300 to $400 billion per year, sufficient to finance all of China's military needs. There is only one proper term for it.

Stupidity on steroids!

The second-biggest sin: competing against each other for China's favor!

The third-biggest sin: continually trying to circumvent public sector policy to gain individual advantages.

The fourth-biggest sin: depending on China for 100 percent of critical or essential products!

If the first sin was stupidity on steroids, then this sin is simply just **stupidity**.

The outcome is as one would expect it. While the Chinese work on a ten-, twenty-, thirty-, forty-, fifty-year planning horizon, unified in its mission, the West has nothing remotely similar to offer.

> ***Unabated, they will achieve all their goals. It is not if; it is just a question of when!***

Besides economic goals, China has territorial goals, such as bringing Hong Kong and Taiwan fully into the fold. Whenever they do it, how little the West can do to prevent it under the current structure.

Yes, there is one available choice: unite in trade sanctions.

Likewise, nobody can do anything about the unchecked expansion in the China sea.

> ***So in the end, indirectly or inadvertently, the Western private sectors of primarily the US and European economies are the best friends Xi Jinping, President for life, could have.***

If the West is mounting large trade deficits, Xi Jinping has nothing to worry about besides meeting all his ambitious plans.

The current situation is a Western competition against each other, best phrased as

> ***"how to best support your favorite 'benevolent' Chinese dictator."***

Good luck with that undertaking.

Have you ever, in the history of humanity, seen a positive outcome dealing with any DICTATOR?

Are there any alternative solutions?

Complex problems require complex solutions. These are the following:

- *The private sector must assess the benefits and harms of dealing with China as a nation.*
- *The private sector must set up a position of ZERO dependencies in any of its dealings.*
- *Western democracies must act as a single unit in their dealings with China and communicate their peaceful coexistence requirements.*

Notes:

_____

_____

_____

_____

_____

Stopping Increasing the Wealth and Pay Gaps between the Rich and the Poor!

We have another similar problem, just as combustive as the "not paying a **self-supporting wage**" issue. Let us call it a talking point par excellence and a red-meat issue for the socialists who aspire to equality for all but themselves.

Let us talk about equality; do we want it or need it?

Equality is the enemy of ambition, drive, competitiveness, and innovation, and it is about the human spirit.

There is nothing equal about it.

Equality is one of the components that kills socialism.

Have you ever heard of a significant innovation or invention that originated in a socialist country?

Yes, there are two: poverty and misery "equally" shared!

So we do not want it ever!

That said, it is not desirable to have a wealth and pay gap, but a gap based on merit. So if we want a difference, what is the answer?

The answer is fairness in the distribution of the rewards our economic system has to offer.

There is nothing wrong with someone becoming a billionaire if others' contributions are not the basis.

Fairness is what we need.

Again, implementing any solution should err on giving more to the lower end of the spectrum, not less. More implies we close the gap, which is good from a public-relations perspective.

Implying capitalists can show compassion, driving the do-gooders nuts.

Let us look at some viable options, solutions!

One solution for a fairer distribution of pay is a simple ratio of the CEO's salary divided by the lowest worker's compensation. The private sector organization can set such a guideline or standard.

That would be fair!

One could envision the same or a different factor for ownership, stock, or bonus distribution.

That would be fair!

We need to be mindful of excessive stock or salary compensations for CEOs, justifiable or not, in the face of minimum-wage compensation for lowest-level workers.

That is not fair!

Another sticking point is the concept of a "golden parachute" for failed executives.

> **It simply is not fair if a fired lowest worker receives nothing and a failed CEO ends up getting millions!**

A general compensation guideline across the private sector would help curb historical excesses.

That would be fair.

Measure any compensation guidelines with a measure of fairness.

The preceding is not an exhaustive list; it is merely a starting point for a more rigorous definition.

Notes:

_____

_____

_____

_____

_____

Development, Education, and Retention of the Future Skilled Workforce

> **Shortages and surpluses of skilled workers at any level should be the exception and not the rule.**

Yet this is not the case for most economies. Extreme contractions/recessions cause surpluses of labor, thus significant unemployment, and in the worst case, amplify the underlying slowdown. In contrast, rapid expansions meet the opposite due to skilled labor shortages.

Neither situation is good.

Please recall, we have started with the assumption of a closed, self-sustaining system.

> *Under those circumstances, all control elements are within the private sector's domain, including a long-term planning horizon for its skilled labor requirements.*

None of that exists today!

So we have skilled labor shortages and surpluses, which is undesirable, but be wary of a government trying to fix this with a considerable risk of unintended consequences.

> *People are not things for convenient warehousing.*

Recognizing the problem, we ought to seek optimum solutions.

There is another problem at the workforce level, particularly for people aspiring for professional jobs. Those jobs require a college education that can last anywhere from four to twelve-plus years. Many students pay for their college education through debt financing, aggregating debt levels sometimes exceeding $200,000.

> *Those debts have reached more than a trillion dollars for the nation taken together.*

If that is not enough, there is another issue for the economy.

> *The mix of professional skills produced by the universities does not match the demand of the economy.*

So there is a trifecta of problems.

> *We have skilled labor surpluses and shortages, excessive student debt, and a mismatch of supply and demand in the labor market.*

So there ought to be a better way!

For some of the solutions, let us look at the public sector. Yes, they do some things correctly, namely and more specifically, leadership development at the various military academies. First, there is excess demand for each offered study place. Second, all students graduate debt-free. And third, all graduates must commit to a specific tour of duty.

It is that simple.

Several questions are begging for an answer.

Workforce education and development

- *What are the education and skill requirements for the entire workforce over a fifty-year planning horizon?*
- *Which industries and corporations need what workforce?*
- *Who defines the required teaching curriculum? What are the essential and optional topics?*
- *What facilities and teachers are needed where and when?*
- *What are the actions necessary to harvest and maximize the disadvantaged and minority potential?*
- *How do we end the necessity for student debt? And more critical! How do we entice students to study and learn a high-demand, essential skill?*
- *How do we end shortages of a skilled workforce?*

Hiring and workforce retention

- *What minimum standards or guidelines does the private sector support for pay, health care, profit sharing, wealth accumulation, and old-age pension?*
- *What are the minimum guidelines for a self-supporting wage for any industry? And how do we assure it?*

- *How do we ensure a sufficient required workforce under shortage conditions?*
- *How do we support our neighboring countries' workforce surpluses?*

Pay, profit sharing, and wealth accumulation

- *How do we figure out pay, profit sharing, and wealth accumulation guidelines across the private sector?*
- *How do we assure compliance?*
- *How do we measure progress across industries?*

Health care and other benefits

- *What is the minimum standard for health care across the private sector?*
- *How is it defined?*
- *Who assures compliance?*
- *What other benefits require a minimum standard? Services such as childcare, working hours, and the like?*

The intent is not to offer an exhaustive list but merely an outline of the undertaking's complexity.

With all that information, what are some of the potential solutions?

- *The private sector must develop and keep a skilled workforce plan over a ten to twenty-year horizon and publish that plan to universities and potential students.*
- *The private sector should adopt the scholarship model offered by military academies to develop professionals and a skilled labor workforce.*
- *The private sector should use workforce adjustment as the last resort method for fighting recessions.*

- *The private sector should control and watch the curriculum taught at various higher-learning places and end one-sided political programming.*

You might pay for Trojan horses.

Notes:

_____

_____

_____

_____

_____

Health-Care Enigma

The left calls health care a human right, and the right favors individual responsibility.

Who is right and who is wrong, or are both right?
Let us look at the implications of declaring health care a human right.

Logically, anything a human needs to survive is a right!

It follows that items such as food, shelter, security, health care, and education are rights.

And if health care must be free, then all other elements must be free.

If society provides all those rights for free, we create a culture with an unintended individual choice.

It leads to unintended consequences, a choice to be a contributor or a noncontributor, a burden.

No society can survive such a condition.

Historically, giving people free stuff is not a good thing.

The concept sounds good, particularly in political speeches, but the outcome is terrible. Let us go back to health care and explore what we know.

Universal health care provided by the government has several characteristics.

It serves everybody, thus has long wait times.
It is highly bureaucratic, thus is complex and inflexible.
And the worst attribute of it all, it does not invent or innovate.
It is resistant to change.

In contrast, health care provided by the private sector has a complete set of different attributes.

It is expensive; thus, not everybody can afford it.
It serves everybody, but at various service levels. The one who pays gets more services than the one who does not.
It is flexible and adjusts continuously to changing conditions.
Wait times are short or, in case of emergency, immediate.
And most importantly, virtually all medical inventions and innovations come from the private sector.
Furthermore, it primarily caters to the working, productive segment of society.

Neither system is perfect! But we know one thing: One is more desirable than the other.

Unfortunately, health care and its various demands and solutions are highly political, with neither party offering a root-cause solution.

For example, the Affordable Care Act, documented in 2,000 pages of government rubbish, came with solutions of $5,000 to $10,000 annual deductibles, while such deductibles surpass the typical annual health-care expenses of working people.

Wow! What a solution!

It proves that good intentions do not always lead to good outcomes.

> *Furthermore, we can conclude, adding a layer of complex bureaucracy on top of a problem does not necessarily solve the problem.*

Now how can an organized private sector solve the problem? *Simplify, simplify, simplify; that is how.*

Many avenues lead to the promised land! Do not get stuck at tried-and-true solutions; those might not be best!

For instance,

> *create access to insurance coverage for all members of the private sector.*

That is simple!

Consider a network of emergency clinics throughout the country, with specific emphasis in rural and deprived areas, which will also supply part of the race and poverty solution.

Consider a two-tier health-care service structure.

Primary and emergency care supplied free to all comers.

Supply world-class care to all members of the organized private sector.

There is a necessary implication from this course of action.

> *Organizing the private sector allows for shifting a significant amount of health-care expenses from the public sector to the private sector, primarily Medicare expenses.*

Wow, there is a tangible way to shrink the federal bureaucracy!

Mind you. Such a solution would consider only a forward-looking change for the sake of simplicity. Additionally, it would enable the public sector to shrink its supporting bureaucracy.

Would that not be beautiful!

Notes:

_____

_____

_____

_____

_____

Pension Dilemma

We all go through three distinct periods in our life cycle. Hopefully, it starts with development and education, reaches a productive period, and ends with retirement or, in unusual cases, a decision to run for president.

The first period takes a long time and costs a lot, but it puts us in a position to become of value for the next thirty to forty years. The last period can be value-creating but does not have to and, as such, requires funding.

There are many ways to skin the cat!

The private sector has had a love-hate relationship with the concept of pensions. For a while, many companies offered pensions. Then individual responsibility took hold, aided by a small government safety net. All ostensibly provided in a boatload of combinations and permutations.

The approach worked well for prudent and responsible peoples. But not so much for the ones on the opposite end of the behavioral spectrum. And there is a term for those.

Old-age poverty.

What we know from the government-run program does not bode well for future generations.

It is not sustainable due to a lack of funding.

And it adds to the perpetual budget deficit.

Both conditions are not extremely attractive. So what is the answer to the problem?

Are there any alternative solutions?

The answer is quite simple.

....

The value derived in the productive period over, say, thirty to forty years must match or exceed the costs accumulated at the beginning and end of the life cycle.
   Otherwise, we are back to the future, which is now.

....

That is why we go broke.
Also, there is another critical consideration.
Payments for the development and education period are **advance payments** *derived from the future expected value.*

Retirement payments are **deferred payments** *from the actual value derived from the productive period.*

So the solution to the problem is structuring **payments** and not being **generous** or **charitable**.

....

So it is a simple business problem and not one of social responsibility as the socialist makes us believe!

....

Under that framework, our business problem is straightforward and does not require a socialist genius like Bernie Sanders and his cohort comrade AOC to suggest a "FREE" solution.

Pension payments or deferred compensation are essential for a stable economic environment and society.

....

We also must recognize the existence of deviations, exceptions from the norm.

....

Any stable system must be able to deal with them appropriately.

We must recognize nonproductive members of the private sector and set up a protocol for them.

One more thing: The private sector ought to take responsibility for structuring and ownership of all private industry-originated pension obligations. That would be the right thing to do and bring sanity back into the looming social-security disaster.

> *Kicking the can down the road or off-loading it to the public sector are not viable options.*

Notes:

_____

_____

_____

_____

National-Security Issues

The private sector is an integral part of the national security solution for the United States. The United States private sector defense contracting corporations develop and manufacture, most if not all, US defense technology. That approach has helped the US to become the sole superpower in the world.

> *Yet in the new and emerging digital age, some developments challenge the wisdom of that relationship.*

Please enter the new Internet powerhouse, **Google**, a trillion-dollar company, as an example that should get our attention.

The Department of Defense approached Google to aid in some computing help for some weapon applications.

> *An uprising within its employees prevented the desired cooperation.*

It is prompting a critical question.

How many of the rebelling engineers are actual US citizens? And how many of those are holders of work visas? The answers might reveal the natural source of the problem.

Google has many "idiot savants" working for them, who do not recognize that their reasonable or unreasonable objections to DOD cooperation are placed at the wrong door.

Ups, we tried to do the right thing! So they say!
Little do they know about the US historical military successes.

Before scaling down US military efforts, one must reduce military expansions in Russia, China, and North Korea.

The US has historically freed people! In Western Europe after WWII and Eastern Europe after breaking down the "Iron Curtain!" Only the minuscule number of about 500 million now-free people. Unfortunately, some Eastern European countries reverted to their old ways, which shows that old habits are hard to break!

No other country has freed so many people in the history of humanity!

One more thing: The US has never taken ownership of any of the conquered territories from its many skirmishes or full-out wars. No other country can claim likewise!

It appears that many of the rebelling Google employees must believe the intellectual nonsense of their leftist professors!

No one could be inherently that naive and stupid!

> *Unfortunately, Google is making a case for government control of the private sector.*
> *The DOD is asking for help, and Google resists doing so.*

Now what could be wrong with that behavior?
Is it arrogance?
Or is it being naive and misguided?

> *Either definite answer is wrong for a free society, relying on public and private sector cooperation for its national defense.*

One more thing.
The resistance or objection by Google employees is justified if, and only if, the US was the solitary country in the world that uses military expansions for its national-defense strategy.

> *However, in the absence of a perfect world, a strong military is the only defense for freedom and democracy!*

That is why all those naive ingrates love to be and work in the US, the most accessible country on earth.
While Google has reached the status of having monopoly power in the market of participation, there are ways and means to throttle the misplaced or irresponsible employee resistance.

> *There is always an "Achilles heel." Google relies to a great degree on work visas to cover its high-tech engineer shortage.*

Thus, it depends significantly on the public sector for its future success.
Cutting access to visas by 50 percent would send a clear message to all those "*idiot savants.*" And it would encourage Google to reassess

its DOD cooperation policies and become a responsible corporate citizen and valuable contributor to the US national-defense efforts.

> *Fortunately, on the other end of the spectrum, we have Microsoft.*

Microsoft is, in many markets, a direct competitor of Google. Microsoft is a more mature company, not only in its physical existence but in its assessment of its vital public, private sector cooperation and in its national defense cooperation and contribution responsibilities. For starters,

> *Microsoft is seeking and getting $10 billion (about $31 per person in the US) DOD cloud contracts.*

Do they have a filter, a gateway that prevents all those "idiot servants" from entering their employment?

Or do they have more common sense at top management?

> *Thank god for Microsoft!*

Go figure!

What is the lesson for an organized private sector?

> *The link between the private and public sectors on national-security issues must be strengthened and not weakened.*
>
> *While in a free and democratic country, the right to self-determination is an essential principle for all corporations, it is also true that the US military assures the perpetual existence of those rights.*

Weakening the military is equivalent to undermining those rights.

Be mindful!
The principal US adversaries—Russia,
China, and North Korea—do not grant any of
those rights to their corporations.

Notes:

_____

_____

_____

_____

_____

Infrastructure Ping-Pong

Decaying, unsafe, or insufficient infrastructure is a problem for any country. If the decision to do something about it is political, then it becomes a tragedy waiting to happen.

Politicians typically deal with issues based on
the "squeaky wheel" syndrome.

He who squeaks the loudest gets the attention. Or he who donates the most gets the attention.
Hopefully not.
Whatever the method, it should not be confused with a plan of action, as it is more like a visit to Las Vegas with not much better odds for finding a solution.

In the school of optimism, a problem for one becomes an opportunity for the other. Given the problem's owner is the public sector, a choice must exist for the private sector. There is another observation we can make.

The private sector is the primary user of all
infrastructure facilities.

Given this to be the case, it makes sense for the private sector to step up to the plate and take full ownership of all infrastructure issues.

And an organized private sector can do just that. Several positive structural changes would result, namely,

- *we have a plan of action rather than political haggling,*
- *we have a constant renewing of vital infrastructure components instead of stop-and-go funding,*
- *we can lead instead of continually try to catch up,*
- *we have a plan and act in anticipation of future demands,*
- *we can innovate because of technological changes,*
- *we have an accountable ownership structure.*

And most importantly…

We get the politicians to stop playing ping-pong with any kind of infrastructure decisions.

Notes:

_____

_____

_____

_____

_____

One-Sided Supply Chain Dependence

The COVID-19 pandemic made it clear that a US reliance on China for most crucial US drug supplies is foolhardy. In contrast, medical supplies in standard times are not an issue. However, when demand explodes via pandemic and the primary supplier, Communist China, faces the same problem…

They distribute all production to their domestic use.
What a surprise?

> *A perfectly balanced supply chain would distribute the limited supply across all participants, thus spreading the pain/shortages equally.*

China outsourced all pain to its customers.

Furthermore, China is not a friendly supplier; it is an adversary on the world stage and may use this dependence to our detriment anytime it chooses to do so.

Remember, the state is the communist party, which controls everything.

Thus, our critical products or services cannot be under the absolute control of Communist China.

Several options solve the problem; they are the following:

- *Diversify the supply chain, domestically or internationally.*
- *Create emergency stockpiles.*
- *Domestically produce ultra-critical items.*
- *Be vigilant and control and check critical supply changes.*
- *Let critical supply be part of a sound export/import policy.*

Notes:

_____

_____

_____

_____

_____

Economic Stability

It starts with a simple question.

Who controls, worsens, or causes economic cycles?

The easy answer, if demand exceeds supply: We get inflation. If supply exceeds demand, we get a disruption on the supply side: high inventories, worker layoffs, potentially a chain reaction of a declining market, and so on and so forth. In the end, we have a recession.

The umbrella organization for the private sector opens other avenues. We can and should look at the problem from a broader perspective.

Let us start with layoffs.

Currently, it is a yes/no solution. There is an in-between solution possible.

Shortening the workweek by half would keep the workers in place while the supply-demand imbalance is corrected.

Germany does it!

What is wrong with copying a good practice?

Increasing unemployment will deepen the recession, while keeping employment high will reduce the size of the recession due to the workforce's retention of buying power.

Are there any alternative solutions?

We can help the economy by keeping employment levels as high as justifiable.

Downturns in economic cycles are also opportunities to train and reeducate the workforce in newly emerging technologies relevant to a particular business.

Notes:

_____

_____

_____

_____

_____

Environmental Responsibility

There is one easy answer to the solution to the problem.

He who creates a problem cleans up the mess.

Better yet, we will have no environmental issues in the future.
Being an environmental steward should never be an issue.

We have only one globe, a globe with limited and declining resources and a globe with an ever-increasing population.

So at the outset, things do not look too good!

Currently, the private sector is lagging behind the public sector in its environmental posture.

And it goes as follows: Public sector agencies, departments, legislations set or define environmental laws or regulations. And the private sector responds with all its options. It either

complies or challenges or circumvents, all depending on the situation.
And it virtually never leads!

Are there any alternative solutions?
Yes, there are! Given the private sector wants to decide its destiny, it must

anticipate and lead in solving environmental issues.

And drop the leading from behind fantasy!

Notes:

_____

_____

_____

_____

_____

Public Sector Restructuring

Is there a snowball's chance in hell to solve the growing **federal budget deficit** and, or better yet, exploding **national-debt** problems?

It is a highly rhetorical question.

Politicians and bureaucrats worth their salt would answer with a resounding YES. But how? Well, this is another matter altogether!

The best we get is "We let you know after we have studied the matter."

And the study will take time.

Let us just apply the tried-and-true Washington practice.
And let us kick the "can" down the road!

What do we know?

We know that one man's problem is another man's opportunity and Washington has a spending problem and there are no apparent cures in sight.

What would be wrong with shifting some of the public sector responsibilities to the private sector?

Consider the following scenario.

The private sector has responsibility for

- *Educating its workforce,*
- *Supplying health care for its workforce, and*
- *Providing pensions for its workforce.*

In short, it is supplying support to its workforce from the cradle to the grave.

Products and services have the following attributes:

- *Are safe and have value-added for its users,*
- *Are safe for the environment,*
- *Are efficient in the use of resources, and*
- *Help others outside our economic system.*

In short, "make the planet a better place to live in."

Given there is no disagreement about the mission, then it follows that several current public sector responsibilities should shift to the private sector. Some of the obvious ones are the following:

- *Department of Education*
- *Department of Commerce*
- *Department of Energy*
- *Environmental Protection Agency*
- *Department of Agriculture*
- *Department of Health and Human Services*
- *Department of Housing and Urban Development*

There are many more opportunities, but they require a little more thought and study as it is with most things in life. In either case, we can conclude that we should review the entire Washington bureaucracy before shrinking, transferring, or ending any of those functions.

The opportunities are boundless and can only lead to a lower federal budget.

Notes:

_____

_____

_____

_____

_____

Is the United States a Racist Country?

Three undisputed facts stare us in the face right away.

With its 618,222 deaths, the Civil War abolished slavery!

Barak Obama, the first Black President, was elected with about 60 million votes, even though the entire Black population is not more than 44 million.

In the whitest of White sports, golf, Tiger Woods, a biracial individual, was the game's undisputed king for almost two decades. Wherever and whenever he played, he drew gigantic crowds of primarily White golf fans.

None of those facts would be true in a racist country.

Next question.

Are there still racists living in the United States?

Yes, there are, as we live in a free country, the most open country in the entire world.

And in a free country, people can do stupid things, and being a racist is one of them.

It is by any measure the price of freedom.

Thus, it seems that the underlying issue is not one of the overt or underlying racism within the US population. It is one of lack of economic opportunity.

Unfortunately, that apparent lack of economic opportunity is translated by racial opportunists or some dim-witted so-called intellectuals into an overt White-privilege issue.

Here we have it!

The White population is suppressing and exploiting Black people!

Unfortunately, such slogans appeal to a broad spectrum of people in the US population, particularly those who want to protest, riot, and loot. Such activity makes them feel good; they have done something about the problem!

Yes, sir!

Given the underlying issue of inferior education, deplorable living conditions, high local crime rates, no job prospects, and no future-earnings prospects, activities such as protesting, rioting, and looting do not seem high on the possible solution list.

> **Contrary to the activists, who seem to believe that DESTRUCTION is the best remedy for the problem, we can conclude that CONSTRUCTION is a much better way toward a permanent solution.**

Furthermore, we can conclude that the cohesively organized private sector is an excellent place to do something about it.

Notes:

_____

_____

_____

_____

Relationship with Religions

Now what does religion have to do with "The next peaceful revolution?" Nothing! Looking at the problem in more depth, we find that there are interactions between commerce and religion globally. Let us look at the Islamic Republic of Iran.

> **On the one hand, they shout, "Death to America," but on the other hand, they want to do business with Western economies.**

They should not have it both ways.

Western economies must set up and agree upon a simple set of rules. Rules everyone obeys for the greater good of humanity.

> *It is hypocritical to talk about human-rights violations individual counties commit on an ongoing basis and, at the same time, engage in business arrangements in support of a better bottom line.*

No pain, no gain.

That saying goes for both sides of the trade, so let us not do it. It is that simple!

What would be some of the possible deal-breaker rules?

- *Countries or regions that support "killing in the name of religion"*
- *Countries or regions that "deny education to women."*
- *Countries or regions that "aspire to become a nuclear power"*
- *Countries or regions that "deny right to exist with ethnic minorities"*

Those examples show that Western economies have the power to bring about change in any of those critical problems. Three conditions must be satisfied to carry out any permanent change:

> *Western democracies must unite and act as one and have a clear set of business requirements, and the West must share critical, essential resources.*

What Next? Can We See the Future?

With all those ideas implemented by our change agents, may we dare to investigate the future, not too distant, but far enough away to not cloud our vision.

Say, let's look into 2030!

Notes:

_____

_____

_____

_____

_____

DREAMING OF NIRVANA!

Imagine Looking Back from the Year 2030!

Much has happened since we all started on the journey, trying to find, understand, and solve the countries' problems. Let us just look and find out what went well and what is not on the macroscale.

What were the most significant and impactful changes?

Two changes had the most significant impact:

- *Forming a workable third party, the Independent Party*
- *Organizing and empowering the private sector*

As it turned out, both were phenomenally successful in turning the country's rudderless ship around and getting us closer to Nirvana.

We all have a notion of what Nirvana is or at least ought to be. Let us just say it is the right place for everyone. Can we ever reach it, Nirvana, the perfect society? Most likely not, but we always ought to try. And those two mentioned changes got us all a lot closer, and that is a good thing. Let us talk about each of those enormous changes and their ramifications in more detail.

Independent Party

Please step back and look at where we had been in the sixties. It was a time of political turmoil and deception. Both parties, Dems and Reps, guilty of outdoing the opposition whenever and wherever. The game was to win politically, never mind the consequences for the nation.

Case in point, one of the most outrageous examples, President Trump's impeachment proceedings orchestrated by the Democrats under a split House and Senate condition. The Dems tried and failed to impeach Trump on his presumed *"close ties to Russia"* first. When that failed, a single sentence in a diplomatic call with Ukraine President Volodymyr Zelensky did the trick; let me paraphrase, *"Can you investigate the dealings of Hunter Biden with Burisma Holdings?"*

That inappropriate phase landed Trump and our country an impeachment trial. Even though, while dear old Hunter made a presumed $850K a year for a job with ZERO expertise, except for being the son of the then-current vice president, Joe Biden, who oversaw Ukraine for the Obama administration.

Now does one not smell that to high heaven?

No, he got the job only for his wisdom and good looks!

The Dems had the House to impeach by partisan vote, and the Reps had the Senate reject the accusations on a straight partisan vote. One deviant in this game on the Reps side had a private feud with Trump on other issues for the record.

It split the country for no valid reason.

....

On the bright side, it showed the country and the world how dysfunctional Washington was.

....

Congressman "Shifty" Schiff lied for hours on end in front of all the TV cameras he could muster. A heretofore little-known political hack from California had the power trip of his life all *"for the good of the country!"*

Or was it for his inflated ego?

Who knows or cares to know?

The *Speaker of the House* and the *Senate Minority Leader*, Nancy, and Chuck did their best to trip up Trump every opportunity they got. Well, that's politics, Washington style.

....

Gone were the times when the country came together in times of crisis.

Recall 9/11. There was no separate Democratic or Republican response; there was only a US response.

....

What was different than on 9/11? Only traditional politicians were in charge!

Trump, the troublemaker, disrupter, was not around then; he came much later.

After three years of constant and mostly unwarranted criticism, a new opportunity arose: blame Trump for COVID-19.

Democrat experts arose on what Trump did wrong without offering a practical alternative. They even forgot their early ridicule of Trump's premature shutdown of foreign travel to the US.

To this day, they give no credit to Trump's masterful acceleration of the vaccine availability in record time, not even dreamed of, via Warp Speed techniques.

He mitigated economic recovery by refusing to countenance total lockdowns that European nations did, with much more draconian setbacks in GDP and unemployment. Sort of like liberal bastions of New York and California did to themselves.

So that was then.

What is it now?

For starters, the formation of the Independent Party did not change the country overnight. Most people confused the Independent Party with the historical appearance of the periodic independent presidential candidates, who were white political noise without real impact. That perception changed with the increasing number of seats gathered over the years.

The Independent voter has a natural home now, and it is not Democrat or Republican; it is the Independent Party.

Now the Independent Party typically has about 30 percent of all seats in the House and Senate.

> *The party differentiates itself from the others as more pragmatic; Republicans are conservative, and Democrats are progressive.*

So there is a home for everybody.

The most significant impact of it all is the change in the Washington mindset. Back in the twenties, it was political posturing for the party's gain, never mind its consequences for the nation. And it applied to both parties. A notable change in thinking occurred because of the presence of the Independent Party.

> *Country first and party second, and not the other way around as practiced diligently by the Dems and Reps in the roaring twenties, not 1920 but 2020!*

The Independents are now the swing vote. Being pragmatic and not dogmatic allows them to do so, and the other parties know it.

So things get done if it helps to improve the country.

That change in basic assumptions rejuvenated the country back to the time the country was born. Now suddenly, everything that makes sense is possible. Let us look at the laundry list of accomplishments; it is overwhelming.

> *We have term limits for both House and Senate.*

No more lifetime politicians!

We changed to a four-year term for the House. No more continuous campaign for reelection!

The maximum tenure for the House and Senate is twelve years, respectively. No more senior fifty-year membership in either body.

We have a balanced budget amendment. No more continuous deficit spending!

And a line-item veto.

We now have a plan to pay back the debt with our surplus budgets.

We have an agreement with the private sector. Both sectors, public and private, will take care of their social obligations.

We have a better defense agreement with the European Union (EU). The EU will build a European Defense Force on par with the US, while the US will reduce its spending to the same level.

However, the agreed joint expenditures will exceed the current collective spending level. So no shortcuts in individual national security.

The US has shed its formerly proudly worn label, "being the police officer of the world," and replaced it with "shared responsibility for national security with other like-minded democracies!"

We have reduced the federal bureaucracy and redefined public and private sector responsibilities to balance the federal budget.

We have moved responsibility for education, energy, commerce, agriculture, transportation, labor, health and human services, and housing and urban development to the private sector while keeping some controlling functions in the public sector.

We have redefined our shared environmental responsibilities with the private sector and enacted a long-term plan to address all critical issues.

We have redefined our relationship with all totalitarian and not-too-friendly nations. Namely, we will help in crises, earthquakes, and the like but will not supply any support otherwise!

The Washington mindset has undergone a near-miraculous transformation, from being a loyal party member to being a problem solver.

The constant refreshment of new blood entering public services serves as a positive catalyst.

One more observation.

The solution to the budget deficit miraculously stopped the growth of the federal national debt.

Surprise, surprise, prudent fiscal management does work!

Notes:

_____

_____

_____

_____

_____

Empowered Private Sector

Here we have an even better story. And it is not the addition of missing structures to the private sector.

Even though we all know that is miraculous, the real surprise is the participation of the vast number of people, from all levels of society, in making this profound change a successful reality—the reality of being an organized and empowered private sector.

Our shared book, published in the 10th edition, has thousands of authors with all these fabulous ideas. One better than the next.

The best way to describe this process is "an organic mutation of our DNA!" All for the better, tiny piece by tiny piece.

Another thought, "There are many 'King' Rudolfs among us!" And they do not require a PhD to participate.

The eluted change began in 2021 with both desired change agents, Bill Gates and Jeff Bezos, agreeing to be a joint catalyst for the most profound transformation of the private sector in US history.

Let me quote Joe Biden at the original Obama Care signing.

"It is a big f——ing deal!"

Notes:

_____

_____

_____

_____

_____

Private Sector Organizational Structure

Adding structure to our phenomenally successful private sector was an easy task. Our Founding Fathers' problems doing the same for the entire country was an excellent guide. They had to create a new nation. The problem here was a little bit smaller as we deal with a country's subset, the private sector. Even though organizing one involved readjusting the other, the public sector.

As shown before, the organizational issues were the same.

A structure of that size requires four components: a constitution supported by legislation, executive, and judiciary.

Additionally, to avoid any confusion, new labels for any of those functions were highly desirable.

The choices were CHARTER for a CONSTITUTION, GUIDELINES for LEGISLATION, POLICY-MAKING for the EXECUTIVE, and CONTROL for the JUDICIARY.

Furthermore, we must have a few definitions to help us create the desired minimum structure.

We all know that it is very dull and uninspiring stuff. So let us keep it to a minimum.

> **CHARTER:** *Control the destiny of all aspects of the private sector operation!*
> **GUIDELINES:** *Help and guide the independently operating components, corporations, and individuals to achieve the desired destiny control.*
> **POLICY-MAKING:** *Define a structure that allows all participants to work within helpful standard guides and rules.*
> **CONTROL:** *Adjudicate deviations from guidelines and rules.*

So much for structure and dry stuff!

Having a structure in it itself is insufficient as there is no life in any of it. Only the entities working within the private sector can bring it to life, which are

- *small corporations, partnerships, and proprietorships;*
- *midsize corporations; and*
- *large corporations.*

Those units are the engines that bring the private sector to life in a dynamic fashion. Small corporations grow and become large ones, and big ones fail and disappear. Nothing is permanent and static, and that is a good thing.

> *Organizing those units in a democratic structure, at a 1/3 constituency, will inject life into the system.*
>
> *It will give each grouping an equal say so, without being dominated by any of the respective groups.*

A lot needs to be said and defined to present a working organizational structure, but this is not the place. Those details would diminish from this book's purpose, which outlines the possibilities for a monumental change in our society.

Notes:

_____

_____

_____

_____

_____

Distributing the Fruits of Capitalism

Let us recall Winston Churchill's phrase again:

> *"The inherent vice of capitalism is the unequal sharing of blessings; the inherent virtue of socialism is the equal sharing of miseries."*

Brilliant as it is, nothing has changed since 1945, since he uttered this phrase in a speech in the House of Commons.

We can conclude Churchill did not think capitalism has a problem, only socialism. However, our experiences with ever-growing social unrest suggest otherwise. And the vast number of continually recurring problems supports this contention.

Thus, capitalism has a problem, which we are trying to solve.

> *And the solution is an organized and "empowered private sector!"*
>
> *A private sector that is in the position to control the destiny of all aspects of the private sector operation!*

Notes:

_____

_____

_____

_____

_____

Reaching Nirvana!

Year 2050!

Now let us go to the fun stuff and answer the question: What did we achieve in giving the private sector some structure? Any accomplishments? Plenty! Let us start with the political aspects.

Independent Party

The addition of the Independent Party transformed the political landscape drastically. Strategic political actions like the filibuster, the House blocking the Senate, and vice versa, the respective majority party blocking all progress, and any other Washington power plays do not work any longer. Two parties could not work together to better the nation; three parties have no such issues. What happened?

The Independent Party is the swing vote on any issue, sometimes in favor of the Dems and sometimes supporting the Reps.

As a net result, all parties are now issue-oriented, as it should be.

Washington now has a balanced budget, thanks to the organization and empowerment of the private sector. Why? There were several reasons responsible for that change in thinking.

Power in Washington is now virtually equally shared as each party typically reaches about 1/3 share in any election. Voters liked the new structure, particularly the Independents; they have a home and a voice that counts—no more being screwed in two- or four- or six-year cycles by the Dems or Reps.

*The emergence of the Independent Party forced
the Dems and Reps to rethink their respective
political roles!*

Working for the good of the nation replaced dirty partisan politics.

Notes:

_____

_____

_____

_____

Redefining the Public Sector

While monumental in their impact and outcome, the preceding actions pale to the federal bureaucracy's revolution and transformation. Only mind-blowing stuff, nothing less. Readjusting thousands of bureaucrats' and politicians' mindsets is comparable to performing hard labor, but less satisfying. The enthusiasm among bureaucrats did not break any records. Yet as soon as all the opposition saw the possibilities, they relented and agreed.

Mind you, selling the individuals on their potential gain makes easy converts.

So it went. All the listed departments and agencies transferred to the private sector with only one purpose in mind.

*Control and perfect their respective operations
for the benefit of the nation.*

It was a noble and necessary goal, but a difficult one. The process was a thorough one as some departments had functions best performed by the public sector. For example, some data collection and control functions in support of a public sector controlling responsibility.

But the most crucial change in the Washington infrastructure occurred as a logical consequence of the private sector mission.

Control the destiny of all aspects of the private sector operation!

So in the end, the following departments went from being public to private in a philosophical sense:

- *Department of Education*
- *Department of Commerce*
- *Department of Energy*
- *Environmental Protection Agency*
- *Department of Agriculture*
- *Department of Health and Human Services*
- *Department of Housing and Urban Development*

Talk about draining the swamp. Politicians and bureaucrats hated it but relented their opposition as soon as they realized that an organized private sector forced them to rethink the entire process and drop their objections. The net result?

A change in thinking of monumental proportions!

The private sector now has sole control of the respective operations, while the politicians kept some oversight.

Without going into the weeds of these monumental changes, some highlights will show the significance of those changes.

Notes:

_____

_____

_____

_____

_____

Human Resources Impact

Let us start with human resources and the associated changes with the private sector. Two rules changed the dynamics of the approach to effective human-resources development.

The private sector supports its workforce from the cradle to the grave, and most importantly…

The private sector recognizes three forms of human resources expenses.

Preemployment development and education expenses, current productive employment expenses, and post-employment or retirement expenses.

This structure allowed the private sector to recognize those costs over any private sector member or future member's life and shift the individual's burden to the proper organization. What would Biden say?

"It is a big f——ing deal!"

The consequences of such a trivial accounting recognition are monumental for all private sector future employees with college or any other degree.

Halleluiah! "No more backbreaking, colossal college loans for any of the new employees entering the workforce."

The new way of thinking, accounting for both pre- and post-employment periods as part of human resources cost, reduced the salary structure during the productive period fairly and rightly.

The other, not-so-noticeable change was the complete elimination and replacement of the benefits for retirees paid and administered by the public sector. The empowered private sector opted to replace the Social Security System and create a more viable, fair, and sustainable structure for all private sector members. Appropriately named,

---

the Private Sector Retirement Fund.

This fund assures a comfortable, proper, and deserved retirement for all private sector retirees.

Notes:

_____

_____

_____

_____

_____

Addressing the Monumental Racial Divide

The other consequence of those monumental changes within the private sector was recognizing that it was time to address its operating domain's racial divide. As shown in the preceding sections, most, if not all, race-related issues have little to do with discrimination but result from **low or no education, substandard living conditions,** and minor **prospects for any change**. In other words, they are the *forgotten people*!

It was clear that those conditions stood for the exception from the norm and, as such, needed some exceptional measures. These include

- *upgrading functional schools,*
- *upgrading or building decent living conditions, and*
- *finally facilitating places of employment strategically near or within those areas.*

> *Expectedly, those measures virtually ended all those "perceived race issues!"*

Let us face it; it was a small price to pay for a unified nation.

Notes:

_____

_____

_____

_____

What about Health Care?

Let us talk about health care, the hot and emotional issue in 2020. In 2050, it is a nonissue.

> *All members of the private sector receive deserving health care, whatever that may be!*

And it is not free; everybody pays a fair share. Enough said!

Redefining the Former Public Sector Departments

It was clear from the outset; structural changes had to occur within many departments and agencies to align the private sector mission with the respective department or agency mission. In simple terms, get everyone to sing from the same score line.

Let us spend a little time on each department's or agency's mission.

Department of Education

The mission of the private sector in education is quite simple:

> *Match future demand and supply for a skilled and educated workforce.*

The private sector restructured the Department of Education to support that mission. The cornerstone of that reorganization was a planning horizon of twenty years for the right skills development and supply to match skills demand within the respective industries and locations.

The restructuring and re-missioning of the Department of Education was the catalyst for the productivity improvement of unprecedented proportions throughout the private sector.

All industries were beneficiaries, with no exceptions.

What were the principal reasons? Was there any sleight-of-hand involved?

No, only common-sense solutions!

It started with finding all youngsters' talents and capabilities and matching those with, first, a development plan. The plan was dynamic and not static to reflect all pertinent changes. And it worked like clockwork.

Both sides of the equation benefitted the youngsters with the best possible profession and the private sector with the most qualified and skilled workforce.

In short, an optimum solution to the personnel problem.

Several noteworthy important aspects appeared because of this rigorous approach.

The Department of Education supplies guidance and needed changes on an as-needed basis.

Execution, such as finding and guiding talented individuals into critical skills, is a local job.

Talent does not end up in the trash bin any longer. It is all about the harvesting of talent! All talent! Not just affluent students or students who attend Harvard and Yale; no, all talent from all neighborhoods.

Now we match talent, educated talent, with critical job requirements.

What a novel idea!

Department of Commerce

The Department of Commerce has several critical missions to perform. Those are to

- *assure a workable current and future infrastructure for all commerce;*
- *find and ensure vital and critical products and services availability;*
- *find and assure no foreign entity controls any of the vital and critical products and services;*
- *manage, maintain, and control the daily flow of commerce;*
- *manage and maintain export and import supply chain structures.*

In other words, the Department of Commerce is the grease that keeps all products and services flowing. Profit is one motivator, but working as a partner with State and Defense supersedes any short-term gain.

The private sector is now a critical partner with State and Defense to formulate and execute foreign trade policy.

The Department of Commerce acts as an enabler for new entities entering and old entities leaving the system with particular emphasis on recommissioning required human resources.

Having set up a sound framework for trade, the Department of Commerce works from a position of strength. All private sector entities are now singing from the same hymn sheets and solidifying foreign and defense strategies for the nation.

What a change from years gone by!

Department of Energy

Its missions are diverse and defined as follows:

- *Assure current and future energy availability.*
- *Restore the environment to its original condition by cleaning up past sins.*
- *Find and develop alternative energy availability as oil and gas may eventually run out or diminish.*

Energy availability in any form is mission-critical for the private sector to function now and in the future.

All forms of energy remain for consideration, including a safe and completely emission-free nuclear possibility.

Dependency on foreign sources is only acceptable if such a partner is also dependent on a vital US product or service.

Environmental Protection Agency

The Environmental Protection Agency has two missions:

- *Correct and end the sins of the past.*
- *Guide the private sector toward environmental impact neutrality.*

There is now a simple rule that governs the overall private sector's environmental behavior.

Keep the environmental impact at or near practical minimum levels.

Concisely, there is no difference between the before and after conditions!

The Environmental Protection Agency does not engage in dogmatic confrontation but looks to find pragmatic solutions to help the nation.

Saving the environment we live in and breathe in is a simple profitable business.

Department of Agriculture

The Department of Agriculture missions are diverse:

- *Feed the nation.*
- *Produce surpluses to help feed the world.*
- *Manage and control ag supply so ag labor earns a fair wage.*

The Department of Agriculture does not engage in strategies that throttle or curtail food production as long as worldwide food shortages exist.

Historical problems of having to use illegal aliens at less than competitive wages do not exist any longer.

The department monitors arbitrarily and unfairly priced farm products. There is little need for counterproductive subsidies.

Low-cost foreign products are not a problem any longer.

We still use some tariffs to ensure no unfair pricing or dumping of import products.

The department works with any capable research facility to aid in the development of more efficient ag technologies. The aim is to conserve all resources for future generations to come.

Be a guardian of all our natural resources.

Department of Health and Human Services

The Department of Health and Human Services mission includes the following:

- *Assure a healthy national population.*
- *Assure fair and equitable pay structure within the private sector.*
- *Assure fair and equitable wealth-sharing within the private sector.*

The Department of Health and Human Services creates and supports guidelines for pay and wealth-sharing across the private sector. It controls implementation through extensive transparent and public reporting.

The exceptional gains in private sector productivity, enabled by the best educated and trained workforce worldwide, allowed the private sector to share its increased prosperity equitably.

Department of Housing and Urban Development

The Department of Housing and Urban Development is, by definition, a temporary entity.

Its mission ceases when race-related economic inequality is a topic of the past.

Until then, its mission reads as follows:

- *Create conditions for successful learning and economic opportunities within minority and/or economically challenged communities.*
- *Create and supply livable housing.*
- *Create a matching job structure within those neighborhoods.*

In 2050, the private sector has nearly completed the task.

Management versus Labor Relations

Labor unions? Most people in 2050 have never heard of that term. Did labor representation disappear completely?

> *No, labor has found its way to the decision-making level at any enterprise.*

What are the consequences of that change? Overwhelming, to say the least!

> *In public institutions, no more hidden and unsustainable pension demands.*
> *No more useless strikes.*
> *No more long labor-management negotiations.*
> *Inclusion has replaced exclusion, and labor is viewed by management as one of the critical factors for the success of any enterprise.*

According to guidelines, the umbrella organization sets the principal conditions of employment, allowing industries to deviate if compelling reasons require such a deviation.

> *The private sector's overall guiding principle, supplying support for its workforce from the cradle to the grave, negates any former confrontational sticking points of detailed labor contracts.*

Thus, there is no more reason for any employee to join a union, which led to their extinction. Additionally, the inclusion concept added to productivity improvements throughout the private sector—a win-win for everyone.

Notes:

_____

_____

_____

_____

_____

Closing the Wealth Gap

Let us talk about one of the socialists' red-meat issues.

The growing wealth or income gap between rich and poor!

Let us go back to 2030; at that time, progressives, socialists, and any other social-reengineering entity you may want to name vilified millionaires and billionaires.

Those were the people with money.

Our social engineers typically had none and thus wanted to "level" the playing field.

While it was correct, some got their riches through unfair leverage and immoral deals; most rich people earned their money legally and lawfully. And what is more important, it created many formerly nonexisting jobs. And if you paid attention before…

The act of creating a job is the most social task anyone can do, particularly an entrepreneur!

If that proposition is true, then the following is equally valid:

Moving a job from country A to country B for strict profit is the most asocial task anyone can do!

It follows that

> *moving a job from country A to country B for profit reasons, while country B is country A's adversary, is the most asocial task anybody can do and is against county A's national interests.*

In other words, if the private sector engages in the latter condition, then those "**profit-maximizing actions**" result in lost buying power in their own country and increase buying power in the adversaries' country.

Nobody should want that to take place, EVER!

So much for the big picture.

> *On a smaller scale, those job transfers without job replacements create social turmoil within the individual, the town, the county and widen the wealth gap.*

Again, nobody should want that, EVER!

Fortunately, in 2050, those issues do not exist any longer. Implicitly, supporting your favorite dictator is a thing of the past.

> *Nobody can understand that corporations could act stupidly on the microscale to make a dollar or two.*

And not be mindful of the devastating implications on the macroscale. Those actions were akin to sitting on a powder keg while lighting a longtime fuse!

The social fuse!

Eventually, the "shit" will hit the fan!

What is the answer to a perceived unfair gap between rich and poor?

If we look at top-management rewards within any organization, there is a distinction between payments for services, salary, and gains derived from stock options and capital gains. In the case of a wage, there are virtually zero risks associated with the payment under normal circumstances, while we have considerable risks related to capital gains. In stock options, we also know we have chances for the potential for high or no profits.

Historically, looking at an employee at the lowest level of an organization, we find a fixed salary, sometimes insufficient for a living, and no stock options. That condition widens the gap between rich and poor.

What can we do to reverse this trend? More importantly, what is the private sector doing in 2050?

For starters, it adopted a straightforward and simple solution in the form of a guideline, namely,

adopt a factor that defines the highest salary divided by the lowest wage paid within any organization and, for example, uses 25 as the starting point.

So if an organization wants to increase the top salary, it must raise the wage at the lowest level to follow the adopted factor. Adopting this method stabilized the continually expanding income inequality.

What about the growing wealth gap?

It was clear that not everybody is sharing the fruits of successful capitalism within most organizations. We also know that sharing ownership is a great and effective way to build wealth. So if we know all that, why do we not do something about it! We also know that not sharing the wealth creates social discontent: people within the system and people systematically kept outside the system.

We furthermore know that systematic wealth-building exclusions lead to periodic social turmoil. What is even more critical; social unrest is either resolved democratically or undemocratically. In the first case, we use the ballot box, and in the second case, we use anarchy.

Neither choice is conducive to a stable nation.

Hence, the private sector adopted guidelines for wealth sharing and, more importantly, wealth building, namely,

- all organizations are encouraged to offer wealth-building programs,
- all employees will participate in the benefits of existing wealth-building programs with any organization,
- all participants have a choice of investments for the wealth-building program to accommodate risk tolerance,
- adopt a factor that defines the highest stock options ratio divided by the lowest stock option offered to the lowest employment level within any organization and use a value of 25 as the starting point.

Implementing those simple guidelines enabled the private sector to stop the diverging wealth trends between the wealthy and needy members of our society.

That is progress for now; yet reversing those trends must be the goal.

Notes:

_____

_____

_____

_____

_____

Dealing with Your Favorite Dictators and Other Adversaries

The historical code of conduct within the private sector was straightforward.

Make as much money as possible, and all things will turn out for the better!

Simple, nothing too complicated!
Such a notion worked in the past; thank you very much, but will this solitary focus on money work in the future? Let us examine the here and now, the year 2050, and find out what works and what does not.

We have an organized private sector with some added responsibilities—broader responsibilities, which require a much broader perspective beyond just making money.

Let us look at a few examples to make the point.

For instance, having goals for agriculture, with its mission to feed the nation and help most of the world, requires a lot more than just making money.

It requires export and import controls for its products and control over all the resources necessary for reliable and safe production, and it demands stewardship over our environment.

So it is evident and straightforward; just making money is insufficient to carry out the mission.

However, that responsibility for a broader perspective does not rest with the individual units working within the organized private sector; it is a responsibility of the governing body.

The respective companies still need to focus on optimizing profits guided by one warning: "Follow the operating body's guidelines."
One thing is sure; there needs to be a mechanism for guiding the individual corporations.

The need for such a mechanism becomes a necessity when we talk about business dealings with adversary nations or immoral dictators.

While there is always a desire to maintain an open dialogue with any of those entities, we should distinguish between keeping dialogue and implicit or explicit support.

The latter should never take place for any reason.
In the year 2050, there is a close tie between the State Department's policies and the organized private sector. Both are working hand and glove together.

The State Department sets national foreign policy, and the organized private sector supports them with coordinated trade practices.

There is always the desire and hope to turn adversaries into allies and direct dictators into retirement.
Past successes will keep that hope alive!

Notes:

_____
_____
_____
_____
_____

EPILOGUE

Here we are, you the reader and I the author. We both know intuitively that all of those proposed changes can and will not happen in their entirety.

Some of those changes have to happen, like both proposed organizational changes, or nothing will happen.

Why, you ask?

Because they are the foundation for all the other proposed solutions and other yet-to-be-discovered ones; the latter observation is an exciting one, at least for me, the author.

Someone else will have to propose a different solution for that to happen, and that is exciting.

Someone, a yet-to-be-defined person, has taken the ball and improved the playbook!

By that very fact, the book has transformed itself from being a bunch of static pages containing a vision to a dynamic entity, an organism that improves by itself.

Now that is exciting.

There is another point worth making. The composite of all the presented ideas does pretend to follow a particular ideology: conservative, liberal, or progressive and the like.

Why would that be?

We all know that each of the ideologies has strengths and weaknesses!

Knowing all of this calls for a pragmatic pick and choosing a methodology that strictly focuses on the desired solution, not its point of origin, the underlying ideology.

A little bit of this and a little bit of that will make it what it is, a unique set of practical ideas with only one objective.

Solve most of the problems addressed in this book.

Is it not remarkable?

Two trivial and forthright changes can carry out all the preceding! One must wonder why nobody produced those ideas.

Too simple, too straightforward, and not too complicated, making it even more remarkable.

Let's switch horses and talk about the here and now, the present. In particular, the current set of either worked-on or planned solutions offered by our people in charge, our current group of politicians.

Let's be open-minded, see what is in the works, and go through some of the most critical issues.

The Federal Budget Deficit

Well, some politicians think they contribute toward reducing the deficit. How? All new spending measures are "**paid for**" by ten-year tax receipt projections. That's how!

At the same time, the debt keeps on climbing!

Additionally, all those unpredictable events emerging like clockwork, as COVID-19, blowing up any budget. And that cycle repeats itself year after year.

So what is the answer?

There are NO serious measures active or planned anywhere in Washington, on any side, be it Dems or Reps, that address the problem.

Yet intuitively, we all know a solution will come sooner or later, one way or the other. The current remedy, printing money to cover the deficit spending without seeing a response in the dollar's value, will not last forever.

May I utter the dirty word, inflation, *and its evil cousin,* hyperinflation?

It is not a question of "if," but only a question of "when."

The Trade Deficit

The trade deficit is a kissing cousin of the budget deficit. If the deficit is small relative to the overall economy, it is not a big problem, in particular if the currency, the US dollar, remains strong. Yet persistent, large trade deficits may create several unintended consequences.

One problem is the large trade deficit with China, a not-so-trustworthy and friendly trading partner.

....

China, a communist dictatorship, can finance virtually all its annual military expenditures with the US trade deficit.

....

That particular aspect might not be in sync with US national-security interests.

Another negative consequence is the supply chain dependency in critical product areas, as the COVID-19 pandemic revealed.

So we got several problems with no apparent solution in sight.

All the Other Problems

Unfortunately, any additional analysis will not change the outcome.

....

*All have a common denominator: No system-
atic efforts are active or planned to solve any
of them.*

....

Be it

- *the national debt,*
- *race-based economic inequality,*
- *shortage of skilled workers,*
- *health care for all,*
- *and the beat goes on.*

So much for now and the present; let's see what is possible.

....

*What are the current solutions to the most sig-
nificant problems addressed in this book?*

....

Let Us Go through a Summary Together

....

*The two significant cataclysmic changes, the
Independent Party's formation and the organized and empowered private sector, were
the catalysts to undo the stale and archaic
Washington bureaucracies.*

....

Independent Party

For one, the Independent Party created a permanent home for the Independent voter who has been screwed royally by both parties, Dems and Reps, in predictable voting cycles.

No more!

The Independent voter can now influence the respective, desired outcomes directly, without disappointment and regret. His party is now the swing vote that counts. The formerly prevalent Washington bickering is only a faint unpleasant memory, only cited by historians and professors as a footnote in history. The sudden power shift started many changes, all for the better if real progress is the gauge.

There were also not such clear consequences.

> *The demand for term limits for House and Senate members is unnecessary if the measurement is cooperation, valid bills created and enacted, and not time spent as a Washington politician.*

Leadership positions are no longer a function of Washington residence time!

> *It is all about effectiveness and productivity; what a surprise and a change in basic assumptions.*

Another consequence: Both private and public sectors are working hand and glove, as they should be.

> *The tool, the Independent Party, made Washington a place for positive change.*

Even at a 30 percent level in both Houses, it reached the position of "**Kingmaker**" by supporting both parties' sensible ideas.

In the "butterfly effect" Washington style, minor changes can lead to a monumental, peaceful revolution.

Race Relations

Another enormous change precipitated by the organized and empowered private sector was the perception of "White privilege" and "race discrimination." It was a sudden, virtually faint change.

> *In the not-so "good old days," like in 2020, membership of a race was either "Black or lily-White!"*

Not true, you say!

Let us look at the facts and see how we classified, not judged, people of color.

Persons with low Black gene content and high White gene content received what classification?

Black!

Thus, we excluded them from **"White privilege"** if there is such a thing.

In an odd coincidence, the progressives and racists agreed for entirely varied reasons.

> *The progressives wanted to expand the deprived class to demonstrate a more substantial number of harmed people.*
>
> *While, as one would expect, the racists strived to keep the race pool clean, i.e., lily-White.*

That perception of race allows only lily-White people to be White! Even though there is also no such thing, all modern people contain various gene sources.

Now we have grown up and classified people's race by their majority gene content.

> *A reversal of political correctness precipitated that slight perception in attitude; we returned to merely correctness.*

Starting with how education allowed the private sector to make a significant dent in the race-inequality problem.

Moving Departments from Public to Private

Why was it necessary to perform major surgery on the established Washington political infrastructure? The easy but unsatisfactory answer is it was the right thing to do. The long answer? An organized and empowered private sector needed more control over its operations.

The most compelling argument for bringing the various departments under private sector control is, in a word, infrastructure!

Let us look at the contrast; politicians talk infrastructure only when it is politically convenient, personally, or party-driven or when the well-known shit hits the fan. Either way, such a method or lack thereof does little to match demand with supply. And what is even more disturbing is, it does not have any supporting long-term plan.

None of the politicians in charge seems to understand that infrastructure is a living organic element that morphs or changes real-time.

Periodic efforts to throw a lot of money at the problem, while commendable, are merely insufficient.

The private sector, the infrastructure's primary user, was, in the past, not equipped to take on that responsibility.

Now it is!

It is the place where supply and demand originate and, what is even more critical, has all the information needed for a long-term infrastructure-planning horizon.

Thus, expanding, changing, reconfiguring, and innovating all infrastructure elements becomes an ongoing process.

> *It is a process governed by experts and not political hacks who occasionally do infrastructure when it is politically helpful. "Do infrastructure!"*

Similar arguments apply to all the other departments; thus, it would be redundant to go through all of them in equal detail. However, there is one element that bears telling.

> *The organized and empowered private sector must control all critical elements of its operation to perfect its overall outcome.*

All those transferred departments contain many critical elements.

Being Socially Responsible

If not all, many of the socially critical issues in 2020 are outdated.

> *The guiding principle of the organized and empowered private sector, supporting its workforce from the cradle to the grave, has virtually ended all the historical, social issues.*

On top of it, it almost dropped the "race discrimination issue," solving social and race-related problems through a straightforward accounting definition.

> *Preemployment costs, employment costs, and post-employment costs guide sound workforce development and post-employment caring.*

Health care, the issue du jour in 2020, is simply an accounting cost entry now.
How simple can it be!

> *No talk of FREE for anything as there is no such*
> *thing as free!*

Everyone understood quite early, social turmoil is not suitable for business, and preempting any underlying issues is in everyone's best interest.

> *Fairness and opportunities were created for*
> *disadvantaged minorities starting with educa-*
> *tion, livable housing, lowering crime rates, and*
> *supplying job opportunities.*

So things got a whole lot better in a brief time.
The racial discontent is at a historical low right now; everybody is happy, except the race profiteers like Al Sharpton.
But who cares!

> *Social responsibility is not local or national; it*
> *is a global issue in a global economy.*

Numerous issues interact on a worldwide scale. Economies such as the US private sector produce surpluses, while poverty and starvation are widespread worldwide.

Populations in developed countries typically decline, while those in emerging countries rapidly expand.

The need for increased food forces poorer countries to cut down their forests, creating world-impacting ecological issues.
And the beat goes on!
What are the answers?

> *The typical answer is to support developing*
> *countries with all their problems, even though*
> *any unconditional help will not solve them.*

It will help to expand it.

More kids, more food!

So there must be a better way!

Help to bring about self-sufficiency while demanding to slow down the population growth rate.

Being an Environmental Steward

Who would have thought of it? The private sector is proud to be an environmental steward and continually reduce its ecological impact with ongoing programs. The unleashed market forces created mind-boggling innovations in optimally using the environment and its scarce resources.

Kudos to entrepreneurs and innovators!

None of those innovations would have happened under the formerly used bureaucrat-controlled government regulation system.

Kudos to innovators for improving the environment!

However, there is still a gap in dealing with the human-made global warming issue.

Conservative scientists still do not believe all the offered data and inconsistencies, while liberals, progressives behave "like strong believing radical Muslims."

Ready to do anything to support the belief!

Call it a modern-day religion of sorts.

It is not sufficient for the believers that the US leads the world by any measure in mitigating climate change. They call for the defeat of all those menacing characters.

Eerily like the Spanish inquisition! It called for punishing the nonbelievers as well.

There is no difference between radical Muslims calling for death to the infidels or crusaders and our modern-day climate activists.

Both are intolerant of other perspectives and unable to discuss a different point of view rationally.

That is why there is a difference between believing and knowing.

One cannot bring about radical change through belief only; one must **know**!

Supporting International Relations

Trade deficits with trading partners who masquerade as friends but are long-term adversaries are no more. Long-horizon goals and targets guide the relationship with any foreign entity, friend, or foe. We know now who we are and where we want to go!

It is that simple!

The State Department is in charge, and the private sector implements the policies within its domain. It is a close working relationship that gets the job done.

The perpetual US trade deficit is no more as the US economy works at peak effectiveness.

Our relationship with developing countries in the western hemisphere is now a mutually beneficial one.

We support all efforts that strengthen their respective economies while they reduce internal corruption.

We now have a very generous program for issuing work permits in the US, thus preventing all those historical mass migrations toward our borders.

....

Illegal immigration is no longer a significant problem; our domestic worker shortages and work permits are balanced.

....

The Trump wall at our southern border is complete. It is a significant part of stopping drugs from entering the country.
So it is valid, after all.

Notes:

_____
_____
_____
_____
_____

ABOUT THE AUTHOR

Dr. Wilhelm Andreas Haberkorn is part of the rapidly declining population that has experienced World War II in person. Not as a soldier but as a child in his native country Germany at the ripe old age of four and five. All followed by the subsequent hardship during the recovery years in the late forties and fifties. The generous contributions of the American people and their implementation of the Marshall Plan converted former enemies into peaceful allies, which shaped the author's worldview and approach to permanent solutions of problems to a significant degree. Dr. Haberkorn came to the US as part of an engineering team to rural South Carolina to create a new synthetic fiber plant. The plant created about 1,000 high-paying jobs for the former textile-industry employees, which changed the social structure in a fifty-mile circle. Minority employees became part of management, even though race riots were occurring in 1968 due to Reverent King's assassination. Another significant experience. Positive changes on the microscale can survive macro disruptions. Back to the author, a three-year assignment to build a plant in South Carolina morphed into US citizenship. And proximity to Clemson University resulted in obtaining a PhD from that institution. Another profound and mind-altering change for the author.

The book *Dreaming of Nirvana or the Next Peaceful Revolution* results from those life-changing experiences.